Deer Diaries

Tales of a Maine Game Warden

By

John Ford Sr.

Deer Diaries

ISBN 978-1-943424-06-1

Library of Congress Control Number: 2015948140

Cover art by John Ford Sr.

North Country Press
Unity, Maine

Foreword

I had the great fortune of meeting John just before he retired from the chief deputy post at the Waldo County Sheriff's Office. John had previously retired as sheriff of the agency, but had returned to help out after the untimely death of then-Sheriff Bob Jones. During the interview for a story about his career, the comedian in uniform rattled off one hysterical story after another. Nothing, and no one, was spared. A couple of hours later when I left — clutching my stomach because it hurt from nonstop laughing — I suggested to John that he should write a book, or go on tour.

Instead, at least initially, he agreed to share his tales every other week in the local paper.

Thousands of people in Waldo County and beyond enjoyed his heartwarming columns about how he rehabilitated Bucky the Deer, Wile E. Coyote and Boo-Hoo and Who-Hoo the owls, and they raced through his heart-pounding tales detailing his pursuit of gun-toting criminals on Moody Mountain.

I admired that in his award-winning, laugh-out-loud columns, John also was willing to share his mishaps — falling off a plane pontoon into a pond, eating spiders out of a bag of popcorn, blowing up taxpayer property with dynamite and soiling his snowmobile hood.

I'm thrilled and thankful John is publishing another book of (mis)adventures. But most of all, I'm grateful for his friendship.

And I do have hope that one day, he will kick off a comedy tour. Or star in a television series.

—Beth Staples
News writer, University of Maine
Former editor, *The Republican Journal*
and *Village Soup Citizen*

Table of Contents

Inspired by a Family of Pros

Game Warden Vernon Walker

Growing up in a family of law enforcement professionals inspired me to follow my dreams. And so I did! I was determined to pursue a law enforcement career similar to that of my family's, hoping to serve the public as well as they had. Pursuing that dream was all I could think about!

That burning desire to become a law enforcement officer was obviously bred into my genes. I vowed to never give up the chase no matter what obstacles might be in the way. Persistence and patience were traits I certainly didn't lack! After all, my grandfather joined forces as an original Maine State Police trooper in 1929, and my dad was a part-time York County deputy sheriff later on in the years. They had laid the groundwork for that exciting law enforcement career I so desperately wanted.

At an early age, I witnessed firsthand the excitement and the challenges involved in a law enforcement profession. It was the anticipation and living in the unknown from one moment to the next that were most appealing to me. Not to mention the adrenaline rush of being on the front lines of real community service and excitement.

Undoubtedly, the two biggest influences responsible for my desire to become a Maine game warden were my step-father, Game Warden Vernon Walker, and my mother, Ethelind Walker. Like so many other families, my parents divorced, amicably going their own separate ways when I was younger, with my mom eventually marrying the local game warden, Warden Vernon Walker.

As a youngster, I found myself living in an environment with several wildlife critters roaming throughout our house. My mother was a wildlife rehabilitator for a variety of injured and orphaned wild animals brought to our house by the game wardens in the area. She patiently cared for all kinds of wild critters, birds, and game.

While most folks experienced cats and dogs roaming freely throughout their homes, we had raccoons, deer, otter, bobcat, skunks, owls, ducks, hawks, otter, and about any other wild critter the wardens had rescued. All of them needed some tender loving care before being returned to the wilderness where they belonged.

I certainly had my favorites. One of them was a young male fisher named Fritzi. Fritzi was a tiny infant when he arrived at our house. It was doubtful he'd survive more than a day or two, especially given his small size and the extremely frail condition he was in.

His eyes were yet to open. His small body fit quite comfortably in the palm of a hand. A steady diet of Mom's tender loving care, feeding him a special formula of milk and other ingredients required to support his small body, became a chore that we all took turns providing.

Those first few days for Fritzi were touch and go—we wondered whether he'd survive the ordeal. But survive he did. Within a few short weeks he was roaming as freely throughout our home as if he were a cat or dog, destined to live with us forever.

Fritzi was a welcome companion upon my pillow at night, as a special bond developed between us. Indeed I was privy to something that many folks were not. After all, how many people could brag about having a pet fisher sleeping on their pillow at night?

Fritzi was very special. He was able to venture outside as he pleased, roaming all through the woods in our neighborhood. Occasionally, he'd return home looking for a handout of grub and a chance to rest.

Fritzi slept on my pillow at night.

However, once the mating season came around, he disappeared for good. We never saw him again. Hopefully he had returned to the wild. This time with a soul mate joining him on his journey.

Another creature that gave us a great thrill was Molly, the skunk. Molly was rescued from a busy highway after the rest of her family members had been killed by cars as they attempted to cross the road under the cover of darkness. Like so many other young critters brought to our home, her eyes were barely open. She was in dire need of nourishment and some of that tender loving care that only my mother seemed to possess. In no time, Molly had taken over inside our house. She acted as if she owned it.

Molly had not been de-scented. She was allowed the total run of the house just like all of the other animals we adopted. Her favorite place to rest was underneath our living room couch. That is, when she wasn't out examining the big world around her. She liked traveling mostly at night.

Molly was quite personable. She loved to be made much of and she wasn't shy about seeking attention. I especially recall a time when a new local Avon representative arrived at our home, anxious to sell my mother some of her new products as they sat together on the couch, scanning the catalogs of the various items she was promoting.

Molly, seeing a new pair of feet dangling down off from the couch, decided to stray out from her shelter in order to investigate what was going on, and gently began poking at the side of the saleswoman's shoes, curious about that strange pair of feet that was easily within her reach.

Apparently the Avon lady simply assumed this minor intrusion to be that of a cat, as she never dropped a syllable from her intense sales pitch, while at the same time reaching down and gently swatting at Molly in an attempt to drive her away from being the nuisance she'd suddenly become.

Molly quickly retreated back underneath the couch. A few minutes later she couldn't resist making yet another attempt to check out those new feet dangling close by. Feet that she wasn't accustomed to seeing. This time the Avon lady glanced down alongside of her. Seeing that jet black silhouette, with a white stripe along its sides crawling out from beneath the couch was quite alarming to her to say the least. The sudden scream was deafening. It was loud enough to blow the wax out of one's ears, as she shot out of the room and back to her vehicle like she'd just been fired from a cannon. Molly quickly retreated back underneath the couch, seeking shelter from the ear-piercing noise that still echoed throughout the house.

I ended up delivering the Avon lady's belongings back to her. Strangely, she never returned to our home again. If I didn't know better, I'd say we were probably placed on the "DO NOT CALL" list!

Thankfully, the loud screams of our invited house guest didn't cause Molly to share a little of her own self-made perfume—you know, that sickening, eye watering, and penetrating perfume that skunks are so well noted for, especially when they get highly excited!

Avon calling!! No more, not at this residence, I'm sure!

By this time in my young life, I was working my way through high school, taking classes that I absolutely hated. The truth be known, I really didn't want to be at the house of higher learning. I simply wanted to be outside hunting or fishing somewhere instead. It was quite obvious that I wasn't destined to become the 1965 class valedictorian at Sanford High School. I already knew what I hoped to do with my life. So what good was algebra, English, chemistry, geometry, or those other mandated classes going to do in making me become a Maine game warden?

The only class I thoroughly enjoyed at school was art. The fact that my mother was a talented artist always intrigued me and her wildlife and landscape paintings were sought-after collectibles by many folks in our area.

I found myself sketching and drawing every chance I got, hoping to pick up on some of her self-taught talents. In the back of my young mind, I decided if I wasn't fortunate enough to become a Maine game warden, I would aggressively pursue a career in art.

Still, I was hell-bent on seeking the game warden career I so desperately wanted. My mind was set. Nothing short of a major catastrophe was ever going to prevent me from seeking the dream job I longed for.

My high school career was progressing ever so slowly as I began my senior year. There was little doubt I was lacking the enthusiasm I truly needed to keep pushing ahead. If I wasn't careful, I might not have enough credits to graduate with the rest of my classmates.

Midway through my senior year, a real crisis ensued after I was caught drawing a rather embarrassing caricature of my chemistry teacher. He was a person I disliked for reasons I never understood and somehow, I was sure the feeling was mutual. The rather unflattering pose I'd sketched resulted in a permanent expulsion from his class and I was ordered to Ike Prescott's office.

Ike, the assistant principal at Sanford High School, was a man whom we students were petrified of. He was a giant of a man who always appeared to be extremely serious and stern— old grouch to be exact! Just the mere presence of Ike scared the bejesus out of us students. You couldn't get Ike to smile if you tickled his buns with a fluffy, fanned out peacock feather.

As I sat in his office awaiting the "wrath of God" the sweat was running down my back. The fear I was experiencing was almost unbearable. I figured that my school days were about to come to a rather abrupt ending, along with any hopes of ever becoming a game warden.

Suddenly the door opened and in strolled Ike. He was sporting that terrifying scowl he was so well noted for. Not one to mince any words, he grumpily inquired, "What the hell are you here for?"

With quivering lips, I humbly responded, "I was caught in the act of drawing a picture of my chemistry teacher during class. Now he's kicked me out of his class with specific orders to never come back," I nervously stated.

Seizing the portfolio out of my hands, he said, "Let me see it!"

My heart was racing like never before. I obviously was in a heap of trouble—big trouble at that! But much to my surprise, Ike burst into a fit of laughter as he studied the drawing from a variety of different angles. Again, this artistic masterpiece was not a very complimentary depiction of my teacher. Instead, the entire illustration was damn-right embarrassing and foul to the eyes.

After rendering a rather heated and intimidating lecture for the insensitive drawing of my chemistry teacher, Ike actually complimented me on the remarkable resemblance in the illustration.

"You tell anybody I said that and I'll flatly deny it," he grumbled, suddenly realizing that he'd just let his guard down to one of his petrified flock.

A quick resolve for this crisis came about with his recommendation to the guidance counselor that I be given a second period of art and that I go apologize to the chemistry teacher for my disgraceful conduct. God bless the man!!! He was not the evil, grumpy, old grouch we all thought he was.

In the end, it was that second period of art and the high grades I received in the class that gave me enough credits to graduate from Sanford High. I wish now that I'd paid more attention to those classes. All of them! In today's world of high technology and requirements, I'd never stand a chance of being hired for that dream job of becoming a Maine game warden.

Pursuing that childhood dream was my top priority when I finally walked away from Sanford High in June of 1965. By the grace of God, and a little help from Ike, I was doing it with a signed diploma in my hand.

The employment requirements for a warden career at that time were nothing like what they are today. A warden candidate was required to be at least 5 feet 8 inches tall; be a high school graduate; 21 years of age; physically fit, and in good community standing after a background check was completed by a department investigator. Those fortunate enough to be hired were turned loose on the public the very first day of their employment. If they survived a year's probationary period, chances were good that within another year or so they'd be sent to a warden school.

Leaving my high school years behind, I was, in the words of Martin Luther King, "Free at last! Free at last!" I was anxious to explore just what the next chapter in my life would be. For now, that dream of becoming a Maine game warden was on hold, patiently waiting for that time when I legally qualified for employment.

Pre-Warden Years

By the Grace of God and with a signed diploma in my hand, my school years were finally behind me. I quickly secured a job at a plastics factory in Sanford. It was a good paying job and covered the bills, but I absolutely hated every minute of it. The hours were horrible with no time to spend in the out-of-doors where I longed to be. Instead, I was cooped up inside a large factory building, a place with no windows, working a swing shift of hours and conditions that were quite confusing and miserable. Many of my classmates were being drafted or volunteering to join the military—the Vietnam War was at its peak during this particular time. Our nation was in a sad state of turmoil and unrest to say the least.

Being somewhat restless and still too young to pursue that warden career I wanted, I decided on a new career change of my own. I planned to quit my job and head out into the world while I was still young. What better way to do it than to join the military, to travel the world at its expense. After all, wasn't that what the advertisements promoted, "Travel the world while you're young—and it won't cost you a dime"?

Against the wishes of my parents, I visited a local Air Force recruiter, who quickly convinced me to sign the papers. In his words, "You'll be joining the best branch of service that this country has to offer." According to him, I'd be able to name my own career field and the places of deployment where I'd like to go. "Just sign on the dotted line!" he anxiously stated. What a farce that turned out to be. His words certainly sounded sincere enough, as I rather excitedly did exactly as he asked. July 20, 1966, I was headed for Lackland AFB in Texas for my first assignment.

Stepping off the plane at 5 a.m., I was greeted by a squad of drill instructors screaming in my ears. They informed us new recruits that life as we knew it was all but over. They had me thoroughly convinced it was! My mind raced like never before. I thought, "What the hell have I done to myself for the next four years?"

Those next few weeks of basic training were spent marching in the blistering hot Texas sun, drilling and marching on the drill field, exercising and doing push-ups on the cracked and dry Texas soil with scorpions watching from nearby. This rather demanding indoctrination to proper military procedures was really not something I'd planned for, nor was I expecting.

Today, I view that brutal training as the best possible life-changing event to have happened to this young, country boy from Maine. I was quickly converted from a rebellious teenage hoodlum into a young man with sound structure and a purpose in life. Those screaming drill instructors had done their jobs, and they had done them well.

My next assignment was at Keesler AFB in Biloxi, Mississippi, for training as a radar operator. We attended both day and night classes, learning the techniques and operations of the very latest radar equipment the U.S. military had at its disposal. During the course of this training, the instructor inquired, "If there were two places in the world where you could go, where would you choose?"

For my first choice I selected a tour in Vietnam with Alaska as my second. The shocked look on his face was priceless when he asked, "Alaska! Alaska! Why in hell would you ever want to go there?"

I boldly stated, "Well, sir, someday I want to be a state of Maine game warden. I love to hunt and fish and to be around wildlife. What better place to do it than in Alaska?"

Chuckling, he said, "Well, son, don't bother getting your heavy-duty Air Force parka out! I'd say, where you're going, you won't be needing it!" suggesting that without a doubt I'd be going to Vietnam.

The war was my mother's biggest fear. The battlefield was taking its toll on so many young soldiers. Some of them were my classmates, returning home in body bags to a nation in turmoil. Vietnam was a very controversial war to say the least. The country was torn between those supporting the effort and those adamantly opposed.

The day when my orders arrived, I anxiously called home to inform my folks of my new assignment. My poor mother was ready to howl as she feared the worst. She soberly inquired, "Where are you going?" She was thoroughly convinced that I was bound for that dreadful war zone.

Laughingly, I said, "Do you have a Maine map handy?"

"What the heck do I need that for?" she bluntly inquired.

"Where is Topsham, Maine? That's where I'm being deployed!" I responded.

Prior to then I'd never heard of Topsham, Maine. Great gobs of guppy poop, I'd joined the military to see the world. Now after a brief stint in Texas and another in Mississippi, and during a time of war, I was going to be stationed barely 60 miles from home! Our government surely works in a mysterious way. This assignment certainly was one of them. To this very day, I'm thoroughly convinced that this assignment so close to home was arranged with God's blessings. It was the answer to my prayers as I pursued that dream of becoming a game warden.

Luckily, during my tour of duty at the Topsham Air Base, I was allowed to take the written game warden exam in the nearby city of Augusta, fewer than 30 miles away. There were more than 300 candidates partaking in the exam process. The odds were not all that great I'd be among the top, especially given my scholastic history! But miraculously I somehow passed, and I passed with a great score. The competition for those seeking a warden career was stiff. Becoming a Maine game warden was a highly sought after career by many young sportsmen. Upon the successful completion of the written exam, the warden service conducted a thorough background check, which furthered my qualifications for future employment.

Inspector Vernon Moulton, the investigating officer, arrived at the Topsham Air Base, where he talked with my commanding officers and the base administrators as to my work ethic and overall demeanor. This was after he had gone through the same process back home with the school officials and many of my former employers and friends. Thank God he never talked to my chemistry teacher! Thankfully, I was given great reviews by everyone involved.

My name was then placed on an eligibility list. Should a position open, I would become available for a hiring interview. I was 20 years old at the time and within a few months of reaching the lawful hiring age of 21. This potential hiring list would be good for a few years. Finally I had my foot in the door, and was one step closer to realizing that career I so desperately wanted.

With a year remaining in my Air Force obligations, the government decided to close the Air Force Base in Topsham. The sudden closure meant we were going to be assigned elsewhere in the world. Maybe, just maybe, I was going to travel around this big old world after all. So much for the thought.

When my orders finally arrived they were for yet another little radar base located in Maine. This one was situated in Charleston Hill, a few miles north of Bangor and a mere 130 miles from home! So much for seeing the world at the government's expense!

Finally on July 20, 1970, my obligation to Uncle Sam was completed. I quickly departed active duty and returned home to civilian life. By that time, I was legally eligible for employment with the Fish and Game Department should an opportunity arise.

Returning to civilian life, I quickly secured a job at the W.T. Grant department store in Sanford as a certified "floor maintenance man." In other words, I assumed the role as a glorified janitor, making $2.25 an hour. Yet another job I truly hated! But at least it was paying the bills. I patiently waited for what I hoped would become a permanent employment position with the Fish and Game Department.

Early one September morning, as I was working at the store, Verne Walker popped in with a big grin on his face. "Guess what, John? You're going to be summonsed to Augusta for a job interview," he anxiously stated. I think he was as excited, if not more so, as I was! The light at the end of the tunnel was getting brighter. I just hoped a train wasn't coming the other way!

The Hiring

Deputy Chief Warden Jack Shaw

Verne was quick to say, "You don't want to go to Augusta thinking that you'll be hired the very first time around. They're going to want to see just how serious and determined you are about pursuing the job. If you get rejected the first time around and you later return when more openings occur, then they'll know you're serious about wanting a warden's career. So, if I were you, I'd simply plan for this trip to be yet another great chance for you to get your foot in the door, and to meet with those who hopefully will remember you during future interviews," he wisely emphasized. Although his advice was a bit discouraging, it made sense. Especially as competitive as these warden jobs had become. Verne was preparing me for a possible letdown, and I was well aware of it.

Thus I departed for Augusta early in the morning of Sept. 6, 1970, for my 9:30 a.m. interview, assuming that the effort was going to be yet another stepping stone in the process of fulfilling that life dream that I'd envisioned. Perhaps the first of many trips.

Arriving at the state office building at 8 a.m., I took the elevator to the main floor of the Fish and Game Department. The secretary, realizing I was an hour and a half early for my interview, tried convincing me to leave and return later at a time when my appointment was scheduled, but I wasn't about to budge. Nothing was going to keep me from that interview, and with my luck, had I gone elsewhere, I feared something would. No siree, I wasn't budging until my time on the "hot seat" arrived.

I watched as a few other candidates came and went. With each of them, I could sense a feeling of success, as they smiled when walking out through the door.

When the hour for my interview finally arrived, the secretary quickly ushered me into a hallway where I was greeted by Deputy Chief Warden, William "Jack" Shaw.

The current Chief Warden, Maynard Marsh, had recently been promoted to the rank of Deputy Commissioner for the agency, leaving the chief warden's position unfilled and Deputy Chief Jack Shaw in charge.

Jack quickly ushered me into his office. I was surprised at the serious lack of space and the lack of decor that was supposed to make it more appealing. But then, who was I to judge? I was equally impressed with the size of the deputy chief. His physical size and demeanor reminded me of Ike, the assistant principal we kids were so petrified of in high school.

Like Ike, Jack appeared to be all business. He quickly sat down behind the large, plush desk in his office, as I seated myself directly in front of him. With very little fanfare or small talk, the first inquiry he made nearly threw me into a panic. Staring at me through his thick glasses that were sliding down over his nose, he smiled while winking with his right eye and he very calmly asked, "Are you single?"

The off-the-wall question certainly scared the hell out of me. It was nothing along the line of questioning that I was expecting. As a matter of fact, I began searching for the nearby exit signs just in case I needed to flee his office. But the only exit was through the single door I'd entered into the tiny office to begin with.

I nervously stated, "Yes sir, I am!" All the while wondering what the heck questions he'd be asking next?

"That's good," he said. "We have an opening available right now. One where we are looking for a young, possibly single, man wanting to make a new career!"

Jack then went on to say, "There are two districts currently available in the state. One is in a remote town known as Daquam. Daquam is accessible only by going into Canada and then commuting down a narrow dirt road along the Maine/Canadian border. There are very few folks living there at any given time. Now I don't think a young fellow like yourself, someone who is just starting out in a new career, would really enjoy the solitude of such a place as Daquam.

"But the other district we now have available is located in the northern section of Waldo County. It is in a region of the state that hosts some of the very best deer hunting country. It also is an area highly noted for its poaching activity.

"I want to be honest with you, they hate game wardens up there in that part of the country. To prove their point, in the middle of the night a few weeks ago, they shot all of the windows out of our state-owned warden's camp, with the young warden's wife and daughter lying on the floor thinking surely they were about to die. The poor souls were terrified, as the flying glass and rocks landed on the floor all around them. Unfortunately, the district warden was away from home during that late hour of the night and it took him and the state police quite a while to get there," Jack emotionally added.

It was rather obvious that Jack was upset by the circumstances leading up to this horrible event.

"Needless to say, that young warden's family no longer wants to live there. We've put the district out for bid statewide for any other wardens looking to make a transfer, but no one seems to be interested. So, now we are looking for a single man. Some young fellow who is looking to make a new start and a career in an area where they might not be welcomed. By any chance is that person you?" he solemnly inquired.

Without hesitating, I boldly stated, "Sir, I'll go anywhere in the state of Maine you want to assign me."

Without so much as thinking about it, Jack smiled and said, "Good, when can you start?"

I thought I'd just won the world's largest jackpot in a lottery! My heart was racing like never before, when I said, "Does that mean I got the job?"

"Well, damn it all, you do want it don't you?" he disgustedly barked.

"I sure do," I smiled. "I sure do!"

Once again he inquired as to when I could start. I replied, "How about tomorrow morning?"

Chuckling to himself, he said, "Why don't you give W.T. Grant a two-week notice. Report back here on Sept. 20 to be sworn in and to pick up your gear. Then you'll have to go to Waterville for a physical before heading off to your assigned patrol area in Burnham. You'll meet with your supervisor Charles Allen and Inspector Lee Downs at the state-owned warden's camp in Burnham, where you'll eventually be staying. They'll work with you on what you should be doing, and they'll explain in great detail where your patrol area will be."

I was pinching myself, trying to see if I was dreaming. At that moment, no words could ever express just how excited I was.

Jack quickly stood up, offering his large hand to shake, as he welcomed me aboard as the newest member of the department. He wished me well and stated, "We'll see you here at 9 a.m. on Sept. 20. Welcome aboard!" And with that, the interview was over. That never-ending dream that I'd forever been chasing was about to become a reality! The long wait was finally over!

I returned to Sanford, completely ecstatic at the great news I was bearing, anxious to share it with my buddies and, more so, my family—especially with my mentors, Verne Walker and my mother. I knew they were sitting on pins and needles, wondering what my day had been like. As expected, they were just as excited as I was, if not more so. Verne couldn't believe I'd been hired on the first go around!

Waiting for the arrival of that day to be officially sworn in was the worst period of my young life. I couldn't sleep at night, wondering what the future had in store, and if I'd meet the criteria expected of me. After all, I was starting out in a law enforcement career in an area where I already knew that I was hated, and I'd be dealing with criminals who obviously weren't afraid to flex their muscles, as they recently had done to the warden's family before me.

What more could I ask for? Anticipating how the reception from the area residents would be and wondering if I'd survive their welcoming were at the top of my concerns.

Would the job be everything I had hoped it would be, or would I be headed back from whence I came, with my tail hanging between my legs?

The Swearing In

I proudly became one of 120 wardens in the state.

That two-week waiting period before I assumed my new duties as Maine's newest game warden was almost more than I could handle. The hours and days were dragging by ever so slowly. After all, I was about to proudly become the newest member of a force of more than 120 wardens scattered around the state.

To say I was anxious to get started on a new career was an understatement. Why was the time dragging on so slowly? It was like the entire world had suddenly come to a complete standstill! I happily gave W.T. Grant my two-week departure notice. The manager fully understood the move and was extremely supportive of my efforts. He was quite pleased, probably more so because recently I'd bargained with him under a little duress by demanding a bold pay raise of 75 cents an hour—a raise that would bring my pay up to a whopping $3 per hour. The highly negotiated bargaining situation came about after an incident that occurred late one evening just before the store closed.

Some deranged individual purposely had smeared an unforgivable mess of human feces on the walls and in the sinks of the men's room. The stench of the carnage was sickening to say the least—one that none of the other employees, nor the manager himself, wanted to clean while it was fresh. Instead, they left this indescribable mess for the "glorified floor maintenance man" (the janitor) to handle the next morning. That was me!

The manager left a note attached to the front door marked for my attention, knowing that I'd find it when I arrived to work early the next day. "John, before you do anything else, please clean the men's room! You'll see why!"

Upon his arrival early the next morning, smiling ever so coyly, he inquired, "Did you get the note I left for you last night, and have you taken care of that mess yet?"

"I got the note," I said, "And for $2.25 cents an hour, there's no way in the hinges of Haiti that I'm attacking what's in that bathroom!" I boldly added. "Before I even consider going in there, I want to discuss a decent pay raise!"

I planned to bargain for a hefty increase in pay long before he walked through the door. Without one, I was ready to hand the keys over to the boss with assurances that I was all done! He could find someone else to do the dirty job at hand! I set the request high, hoping he'd meet me halfway. "I'm looking to get another 75 cents an hour," I said.

I was shocked when he quickly said, "OK, we certainly can do that. Now, would you go clean the men's room and get it back into shape as soon as possible?"

"Damn it all," I sputtered to myself, "I sold myself too cheap." I knew damn well I should have been asking for more. Much more!

In the end, I got that pay raise I'd asked for, and now two weeks later I was leaving the store for good. I'm sure the manager was quite relieved, recognizing the fact that he'd be able to hire someone new to assume my duties. Probably at my old rate of pay, and as a result he'd be saving the store a few bucks in the process. At least for the time being, I had held my ground. As a result, I got to reap the rewards of my bargaining efforts in only one paycheck before leaving the store's employment.

I hardly slept a wink the night before I was to make the journey north to be sworn in as the state of Maine's newest game warden. The hype and anticipation were almost more than I could stand. I awoke early that morning. Verne and my mother were already awake and I could tell they were as excited as I was. They had prepared a warm breakfast—one fit for a king— before I was to head out for the north country.

Verne was rapidly passing along a barrage of bits and pieces of well-intended advice. He wisely advised this baby warden as to what I should be watching out for and what I shouldn't be doing—what I could expect for activity in the days and months ahead and, most importantly, he advised me to always be watching my backside.

Verne was genuinely concerned about passing along the very best advice he could muster—and I was eternally grateful to be receiving it. The list was endless as he went from one subject to another, emphasizing the fact to "not take the job personally. But to instead, enjoy every minute of it, including those times when those folks you'll be dealing with will brag about pulling the wool over your eyes," which he assured me they'd do!

"And just remember," he spouted, "they shot deer illegally up in that country long before you got there. They'll shoot deer illegally while you're there, and they'll shoot deer illegally long after you're gone, so don't think you're Marshal Matt Dillon, ready to clean up Dodge City, because I can tell you right now, it ain't gonna happen!"

"Through it all, they'll keep trying to play a cat-and-mouse game with you. Don't take it personally! It's not you they despise, but it's the badge you wear and the profession you are in. You're a real threat to their existence," he wisely warned, as we feasted on a meal of bacon and eggs as we all sat around the kitchen table.

"Try to treat those people with the same respect you'd want for yourself, no matter how bad they try to insult or belittle you. If you can do that, John boy, eventually you'll get that respect back," he emphasized. All of these comments were appreciated far more than he knew.

Verne was like an old tired rooster, ready to send a young cock out into the hen house to assume his duties, as he intently watched and observed the actions from way off in the distance. Perhaps the best advice Verne passed along, however, was that of keeping a daily diary or a log.

"Keep a log of those events and those incidents that you'll want to remember the most regarding your career," he stated. "If you do that on a regular basis, who knows, maybe someday you'll write a book, sharing those great moments and experiences with the public. I wish to hell I'd done it during my time, but I never did!" Little did I know at the time just how valuable those words and that advice would become.

After a great meal at home, it was at the crack of dawn that I found myself heading north for the beginning of a brand new life. The fulfillment of a dream come true!

Deputy Fish and Game Commissioner Maynard Marsh, who recently had been promoted from his position as the chief warden, quickly administered the oath of office. He swore me in as the newest "baby game warden" to represent the state of Maine. With no fanfare or witnesses to view this proud moment of my life, I was officially inserted into the history books as the newest member of the Maine Warden Service.

Sept. 20, 1970 - The Big Day

I signed countless pieces of paperwork regarding my new career. There were several forms pertaining to payroll, insurance, retirement, medical, and several other aspects involving my new profession. Quickly signing the papers, one right after another, I barely read or understood any of them. Truthfully speaking, I didn't care. I simply wanted to get started on my life's new adventure. All of that damned old paperwork wasn't a top priority as far as I was concerned.

The next step in the process was a trip to the department's storehouse on Federal Street in Augusta to receive the uniforms and equipment I'd need to perform my duties. I got sleeping bags, uniforms, coats, boots, firearms, gun belts, handcuffs, ammo, binoculars, hats, summons books, notebooks, flashlights, topographical maps, compasses, and more. The list was endless and especially exciting when it came to picking out the big items, such as a cruiser, a boat, and a snowmobile. I felt like a contestant on a television game show, one where I'd just picked the lucky curtain, winning the grand prizes stashed behind it. It was an overwhelming experience to say the least.

Wendell Symes, the storehouse supervisor, quickly outfitted me with several sharp-looking uniforms. "Your Supervisor Charlie Allen, will give you your badges when you meet with him later on today," he rather bluntly and unemotionally stated.

Wendell was a rather strict and right-to-the-point type of fellow. His brashness in the overall operations of the warden service storehouse earned him the title of "Tiger" by most of the wardens out in the field. Once Tiger heard I was the stepson of Warden Vernon Walker, his attitude changed drastically.

"Your stepfather is one of the nicest men I've ever met," Wendell humbly stated. Of course, I had to agree that he certainly was. "You have some real big shoes to fill there, son, if you are to measure up to half of what Verne and the other wardens in this state have accomplished during their careers." He was absolutely right, there was no arguing that issue!

Wendell's assistant at the storehouse was a civilian lady, Linda Perry. Linda took her job very seriously. I actually viewed her as being the real Tiger of the outfit. She obviously was in control and absolutely no one was about to short change her, especially some new rookie warden. Nothing was going to leave from inside that storehouse that she wasn't comfortable issuing.

Linda's large frame and tall stature, along with her authoritative voice, certainly got my attention. She reminded me of those drill instructors I'd experienced in basic training. I couldn't tell if she liked me or not, but I soon learned that she was "all bark" and "no bite." In time, I'd get to test her so-called authority in ways I might later regret!

Completely outfitted with a slew of brand new equipment and supplies, all of it carefully packed inside the cruiser I'd be driving, I was ready to continue the trek northward. I had to make a brief stop at Thayer Hospital in Waterville to meet with Dr. Sullivan, the department's physician, who administered a quick physical, authorizing me as being totally fit for employment. Maine's newest "baby game warden" was finally headed for his new career in Waldo County!

Let the stories begin!

Grampy and the Kid

Upon my arrival at the Burnham warden's camp, I was cordially greeted by my new bosses, Warden Supervisor Charles Allen, Inspector Lee Downs, and District Warden Norman Gilbert. Supervisor Allen proudly pinned the badge on my uniform, welcoming me into the division, as we went over the many reports and the paperwork I was expected to complete. At the same time, they discussed what they expected from me as their newest employee. Warden Gilbert from Hartland, whose patrol district bordered mine from the North, was assigned by Supervisor Allen to be my working partner.

"Norman will be working with you, showing you the district lines and the areas of coverage you'll be responsible for," Charlie stated. "You two will be partners!" he emphasized.

The department wanted wardens working in pairs as much as possible, especially when confronting those night-hunting desperadoes who defiantly challenged the hunting laws. Working with partners made complete sense, considering the fact that these night-hunting folks were armed to the hilt and often motivated by a little alcoholic beverage. After all, one man alone attempting to arrest a carload of armed and drunken bandits in the middle of the night, especially in the remote countryside, could find himself in a bad fix. Especially without anyone to witness or assist him in his enforcement efforts.

Norman was nearly 30 years older than I and obviously much wiser than this rookie warden he was taking under his wing—a point he strongly stressed to yours truly right from day one! It was obvious the old boy relished his command of a new recruit, and he was going to take full advantage of it.

Warden Norman Gilbert

Due to the discrepancy in our ages, we were quickly dubbed "Grampy and the kid" by the other wardens working in our division. After a little time had passed and we became well acquainted, I occasionally referred to us as "Grumpy and the kid," especially after I'd committed some act of defiance that caused Norman to get that proverbial "hair across his rump!" Those incidents usually resulted in a pouting session between the two of us. Anyone watching from the outside would think that we were having a lovers' spat! Of course, I'd never admit to any wrongdoing, which usually made the "old goat" madder than a cluster of yellow jackets on the war path.

Whenever he spoke, Norman's French/Canadian heritage was quite evident. His small, rather petite 5-foot-8-inch frame, accompanied by a balding head and a weathered face, reminded me of a small porcupine with a few short quills protruding from the top of its head. His laugh was unmatched by anything I'd ever experienced before. It was similar to a small squealing pig being manhandled at a country fair during a pig scramble by a bunch of rambunctious teens.

Norman constantly carried a plastic jug of warm milk with him in the cruiser. Whenever situations got a little stressful or hectic, the warm milk was his crutch to smooth things out. Supposedly it made him feel more secure. He claimed the warm milk fed an ulcer he supposedly had. Whether he actually had one, we never knew.

It was almost comical watching Norman at the conclusion of some bizarre incident, or after some tense and stressful situation, as he poured the warm milk down his gullet, trying to ease his fragile nerves.

More often than not, it would dribble down his chin and onto his uniform. I knew damn well that in the days ahead I'd probably witness him going through more of that "cow juice" than any time before in his lengthy career.

Working night after night, day after day, seven days a week in the fall, provided us a great opportunity to personally get to know each other. Through it all, we bonded in a strange way, with both of us thoroughly enjoying our careers. Norman became part of my family, and I did his, as we spent countless hours working and sharing so many experiences together.

Some of those more memorable moments, the many times when the milk jug was tipped up and the excitement prevailed, I decided to share in this book. I have to admit, they certainly were good times!

Beneath the Heavens

Don't ask me why, but there was something majestic about spending the cold and frosty nights underneath the stars, while listening to the howls of a nearby pack of coyote, or the hoots of an owl, as the falling stars lit up the heavenly skies high overhead. Working under those conditions was quite enjoyable and oftentimes highly entertaining, as we sat patiently waiting for a group of night hunters to venture our way. We often saw sights, and heard sounds, during those late-night hours that most folks never dreamed of, simply because they were peacefully resting within the comforts of their own beds.

Occasionally, the quiet night air was shattered by a gunshot blast off in the distance, indicating that someone was pursuing a deer that had suddenly been hypnotized by the bright beam of light being cast into its eyes and then killed by the ensuing rifle shot. To pull up stakes from where we sat, in hopes of chasing shots to catch the culprits involved, was a waste of time. The damage had already been done and the perpetrators were more than likely long gone by the time we were able to locate the scene of the illegal activity. Persistently staying parked in a location, especially at a place where the deer were plentiful, hopefully would lure those same people to our location.

With the lights of each approaching vehicle, the tension and anticipation mounted. Is this the one we are looking for? It was kind of a mental rush, hoping to surprise these lawbreakers by catching them red-handed, in the act of committing their cardinal sins. However, most of the cars passed on by, totally unaware of our beady little eyes watching their every move.

As the evening got later, our chances of success became greater. For the most part, a night hunter tried to commit his dastardly crime when the traffic was at its lowest and the chances of anyone seeing them were rare. In the meantime, we feasted on snacks of popcorn, doughnuts, sandwiches and other goodies, all of it downed with a swig of Moxie, or hot coffee, warming up the innards.

The biggest problem that confronted every one of us, was trying to stay awake, especially if we'd been working all day with little or no rest. Maintaining a chaotic work schedule constantly took its toll as far as being able to stay awake and alert. We'd try all kinds of tactics to overcome the urge of falling asleep—everything from leaving the windows rolled down to circulate a flow of cold fresh air into the cruiser, to actually rolling out the sleeping bag on the hood of the cruiser where we could hear and see more of what was going on around us. I doubt the general public had a clue of how many hours we wardens spent in the field during the night. All of it perched in one area, patiently waiting for a poacher to come our way! The cat-and-mouse game was on. Norman and I were the two cats, each of us sitting underneath the heavens, anxiously waiting for the mouse to approach the bait!

Even those small herds of whitetails, foraging in the dark all around us, were completely unaware of our presence. Time was on our side as to catching these night-hunting culprits, but it was luck that we needed more than anything else!

Trash Can Patrol

It was an extremely damp, cool, and foggy October night in 1970 when Norman called my residence, demanding that we meet in the town of Pittsfield to decide what direction we'd head off to in order to watch for those dastardly night hunters. Sitting beneath the street light in front of the Pittsfield police station, I couldn't believe we were even considering the possibility of working night hunters on this particular evening, as the fog was so thick you could almost slice it with a knife. We couldn't see four feet in front of us.

"Norman, we have to be completely nuts to think any damned fool in his right mind would be out night hunting tonight! You can't even see the hood of your car for God's sake!" I sputtered.

"Mmmm, you might be right."

I knew it would have to be his call to cancel the evening. God forbid I should even suggest the thought—he'd do just the opposite just to be spiteful. Norman had to be the one calling all of the details and certainly not some rookie warden who was just starting his career.

"I think we'll do something a little different tonight!" he suggested, with a big grin on his weathered face.

"What's that?" I inquired.

"We'll go out onto the interstate and head down to the rest area, seeking a little entertainment," he deviously snickered.

"What the hell kind of entertainment is out there?" I inquired.

"You'll see!" he smirked. "But you have to promise to keep it a secret," he added.

I couldn't for the life of me imagine what could be so entertaining at the rest area, especially on such a foggy night when you couldn't even see 10 feet in front of yourself. But regardless of what I thought, it looked like I was about to find out. We shot out of town and out onto the busy interstate highway, headed for the rest area a few miles away.

Pulling into the fog-covered parking lot, Norman scanned the area for vehicles.

"I'm going to let you in on a little secret," he smirked, as he brought the cruiser to a sudden stop. "This rest area is often used by the truckers traveling all over the country and by those who are just now returning home after a week or two out on the road. They often will stop here to clean out their vehicles before returning to their wives, after a long cross-country road trip."

Still unable to envision just what the hell he was talking about, I numbly said, "So, what's your point, Norman?"

"You take your flashlight and you start searching all the trash cans at one end of the parking lot and I'll do the same at the other end," he smiled.

"What the heck are we looking for?" I numbly inquired, wondering if perhaps my partner hadn't completely lost his mind.

"Many of these cross-country truckers will stop at adult bookstores during their travels, buying stacks of porno magazines to entertain themselves while they are out on the road," he snickered. "They don't want their wives to find the magazines, so they stop here, disposing of them before they get home! You ought to see the collection I've built up over the years," he laughed.

Who would've believed that two of Maine's finest game wardens would be engaged in garbage can patrol at a rest area on Maine's busiest highway? Norman was like a little kid at an Easter egg hunt, as he cautiously monitored the parking lot for incoming traffic, while thrashing through the garbage cans seeking magazines for his private collection.

I followed his moves, to see if in fact he knew what he was talking about. He certainly did! The old boy obviously was well aware of the happenings within his district. I could vouch for that! He knew his people and their every move! Much to my surprise, the cans produced a hefty supply of the smut magazines he'd raved about. I couldn't believe it.

We completed the mission we were on and, armed with a bundle of the recovered magazines, we drove back to the bright street light in front of the Pittsfield police station. Together we began scanning and comparing the cache of smut, straight out of the trash cans from the local rest area.

Now, I don't mean to let Norman's little secret out of the bag, because I already did at his retirement party many years ago, in a fun-filled roast of the old boy's illustrious career. I revealed his little well-kept secret to all of his friends at a retirement roast, accompanied by a self-drawn cartoon depicting the garbage can event, along with several other happenings over the years. All of them drew an enthusiastic laugh from his many friends, co-workers, and family in attendance.

In order to make his roast more memorable, I made him sit directly in front of his cronies as page by page I slowly flipped the many cartoon caricatures I'd assembled for this memorable event. It was done with the best intentions of showing how well we had bonded over the years and moreso, recalling the great times we both had shared throughout our careers.

It was indeed a sad day when Norman decided to pull the trigger and walk away from the illustrious career he so loved in the late 1980s. Thirty-three years of warden work—and now in the blink of an eye it was over. We both would miss the crazy times and the many laughs we shared between us, not to mention a few hair-raising moments along the way.

Displaying those cartoon drawings brought back that horrid memory from my high school years and the drawing I'd made of my chemistry teacher that got me bounced out of his class for good! Old tricks were hard to break and this drawing stuff was one of them!

It was a night to remember for sure. All of it in fun!

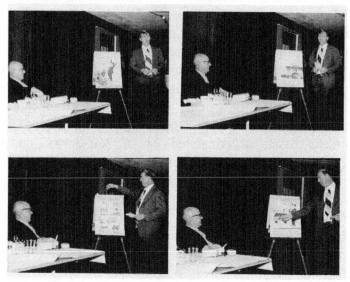

Roasting Warden Gilbert at his retirement party

The Flying Hairball

I especially recall one of the more memorable moments when I was working with my partner, Norman. This incident occurred on an unusually warm fall night in 1971. We were parked in a farm yard in an area Norman knew well. It was a typical old barnyard, with cow manure piled up everywhere, along with a display of broken down equipment scattered all about the yard and the usual cluster of barn cats and chickens milling about the clutter.

Down the road from where we sat, were several green fields, including a grove of old apple trees that made a great habitat for the deer. The area had been subjected to a little night hunting in the past, so Norman thought we should give it a little attention on this warm Indian summer fall night.

We parked the cruiser alongside of the dairy barn, in a spot where we could observe the goings on around us. I was completely exhausted from working several days and nights in a row. Norman, on the other hand, had a daily ritual that he followed faithfully and without exception. He was home taking a nap every day, from early in the afternoon until supper time, so he could be alert for the evening patrol. On more than one occasion he ripped me a new set of jeans because I'd fallen asleep during the midnight hours. He supposedly had to do all the watching, as I lay in a comatose state alongside of him. He was totally unsympathetic of the many hours I was working, while he was resting at home every afternoon, sound asleep in a comfortable easy chair.

On this night I'd already slouched down on my side of the car, ready to drift off into la-la-land, as Norman sat on his side of the cruiser, grumbling about something I was barely listening to. Obviously whatever the topic had been, in my view it was something that didn't amount to a tinker's damn! Norman was sprawled out behind the steering wheel, with his window rolled completely down and his arm resting comfortably outside. As he continued sputtering away, I drifted off into never, never land, barely coherent to anything going on around me.

Suddenly, there was this God-awful screeching and thrashing next to me. The chaos caused me to immediately pop my eyes open from that deep sleep I'd drifted off into only minutes before. I glanced over at Norm, just in time to see this huge, furry hairball scaling through the air headed my way. In self-defense, I quickly raised my arms, deflecting the fuzzy invader onto the dashboard of the cruiser. Scrambling wildly, it screeched at the top of its lungs and dug four feet into the dash. The fur ball then shot back into Norman's lap and straight out through the window from whence it had come.

All of this happened in a split second. Norman frantically opened the cruiser door in a mad attempt to escape the impending danger of the creature. I'd already fled as far away from the vehicle as I possibly could get. Norman huffed and puffed and leaned up against the side of the car, desperately trying to maintain his composure. The warm milk was already streaming down his chin and onto his uniform.

I was yelling, "What the hell was that?" as I watched Norman tilt the milk jug upwards for yet another fix—one that he desperately needed. He appeared as though this was going to be his last drink and the only chance for his survival!

"It was one of those gawd-damn cats, I think!" he growled, as the milk flowed freely down his chin. "Damn things, I never did like them!" he disgustedly sputtered.

After the madness and chaos of the moment had calmed down, we pieced together just what had happened. Apparently one of those barnyard cats had climbed up onto the roof of Norman's car as we sat idling in the barnyard. In an attempt to get back onto the ground, it jumped from the roof, landing squarely on top of Norman's outstretched arm. By then, Norman had drifted off into his own little world in tinsel land, as he lay comatose on his side of the car. When the cat landed on his arm, as a matter of self-defense, he quickly snapped his arm back in through the open window. The cat, firmly attached to his arm, came scrambling directly my way. The cat shot back out through the window as quickly as it had come in, almost as if someone had painted raw turpentine on its rear end.

Yet another great night out on the job, never knowing just what dangers lurked ahead. In the end, we both shared a good laugh, with Norman keeping his window closed for the remainder of our stay in the old farmer's dooryard. I bet that old cat will never forget the night when we temporarily invaded and he became a flying fur ball within the security of his own domain among the cow manure, the wandering chickens, and the other cats of the farm yard.

One thing was for sure—we never forgot that night!

You Damned Peeping Tom, You!

On Oct. 31, 1971, I was still a young rookie learning the ropes from my working partner. Norman rather excitedly called my residence, demanding that I head for his house to assist him with a complaint he'd just received.

"Don't let any grass grow underneath your feet getting here!" he barked.

Whenever Norman wanted something done, it was right then and now. Not one minute later, especially if he was excited, as he appeared to be on this morning. As usual, he wouldn't divulge what we were going to be working on, or where we'd be going. That was his subtle way of keeping me in suspense, so that I'd expedite my travels and not dilly-dally along the way.

When I arrived at his dooryard, Norman was anxiously waiting with his red jacket and a jug of warm milk in his hands. Jumping into my cruiser, he shouted, "Head for the town of Harmony," as he rambled on about having received some real reliable information regarding an old poacher named Arnold in his district.

Arnold had been on Norman's "most wanted list" for a long time. He was well known within the region as being one of the more notorious night hunters living in Norman's area. Arnold's house was located on a back country road, a short distance out of town. According to Norman's information, Arnold and a couple of his drinking buddies had gone on a major night-hunting spree the previous night, illegally bagging four deer in the process. The informant, who just happened to be the disgruntled wife of one of the participants, stated the deer that were illegally harvested were hidden underneath an old wooden door placed over a large hole in the ground behind Arnold's house. The plan called for them to move the deer later in the day, after they managed to get a little rest from the night-hunting excursion that found them cruising and hunting into the wee morning hours.

"That gawd damn Arnold has gotten away with this type of activity for years," Norman griped. "By the Jays-us, today we are going to slap our meat hooks into him, John boy," he bragged. At the same time he was constantly tipping the milk jug up to his lips. The white cow-juice was flowing down his chin and onto his uniform as it always did whenever he was in a rush for a quick fix.

"I've been waiting a long time for this John boy! I want to bag this son-of-a b—, and today he's gonna be all mine! I'll show Arnold he isn't so damned smart as to what he thinks he is!" Norman boldly sputtered. The adrenaline-pumping display of sheer emotion coming from my partner was quite a show for this rookie warden. All the while, I was wondering just what kind of a mess we were about to get into.

At the residence we were greeted by a shady-looking character. His grayish hair was long, shaggy, and matted, and he was sporting a scruffy beard covered with a thick layer of yellow tobacco stain. From all appearances it looked as if he had just crawled out of bed.

Norman whispered, "That's Arnold!" as we approached the man standing in the doorway. "He looks like he's still exhausted from his long night out on the town," Norman grumbled.

Arnold's residence certainly wouldn't have won the award for most beautifully kept house of the year in a Better Homes and Gardens contest. The dooryard was completely littered with several old junk cars. There were rusty pieces of machinery scattered all around the property, with thick mounds of grass growing up between them. Chained to a nearby fallen down shed were a couple of baying coon dogs, surrounded by piles of dog feces. The hounds were loudly howling at our presence within their dooryard.

From all appearances, the household garbage was simply being tossed out through the shed door and into a pile alongside of the house. Several windows in the home were broken and simply boarded over or covered by cardboard. The few panes of glass that were still intact were so filthy you couldn't possibly see through them.

The fallen down shed was decorated with several bleached-out deer antlers nailed onto the outside walls, obviously displaying trophies from years gone by.

Without beating around the bush, Norman boldly said, "Morning, Arnold. I've been told you've got some illegally killed deer stored around here and we've come to pick them up."

Arnold said, "Oh really, Norman! What damn fool has told you that bunch of hogwash? You, of all people, should know that it's highly illegal to possess a deer this time of year! You do know that, don't you, Norman? Surely, you don't think I'd be stupid enough to poach one, do you Norman?" he sarcastically muttered.

Norman wisely responded, "Arnold, what I think really doesn't matter, does it? If you don't have any deer around here, then I'm sure you won't mind us looking around, will you?"

"Ain't no deer here, Norman! But if you want to look around, you just go right ahead! I'm going back to bed because I really don't have time for your damn foolishness!" Arnold shouted at the top of his lungs. "You're not going to find anything," he bellowed as he slammed the door in our faces.

Out behind the house was the wooden door laying on top of the ground, just exactly as Norman's informant had described it. Sure enough, stashed in a hole beneath it, were four freshly killed deer, all piled on top of each other.

Norman began to hyperventilate with excitement, "Looky here, John boy, looky here! You stay right there, and don't you let anyone near these critters. I'm going to get Supervisor Nash headed this way to assist us!" he excitedly sputtered. "I've got a feeling Arnold ain't gonna be too happy and cooperative from this point on," he said, as he shot across the lawn heading for the cruiser, requesting assistance from the boss.

While Norman sat in my cruiser calling on the radio for the boss to arrive, I watched from afar as he guzzled almost his complete supply of warm milk.

"Supervisor Nash and Inspector Downs are headed our way John boy," Norman yelled from inside the cruiser. "I'm going to stay near the radio to guide them in. You stay right there and don't you let anyone near them damn deer!" he shouted in that dictator tone of voice that he so often used whenever he felt he was totally in charge.

Now mind you, I was new at these investigative techniques. This was my very first really big poaching case. I was relying upon my partner's many years of experience to guide me, as I obediently stood alongside of the illegal carcasses, guarding them as if they were gold coins hidden behind the doors of Fort Knox.

Suddenly, I saw Arnold hiking across the lawn with fire shooting out of both eyes. He was headed my way like an angry bull charging a bright red blanket. The steam was shooting out of both of his nostrils as he charged forward, yelling at the top of his lungs, "You gawd damn sick fish cop! You get the hell out of here right now! You perverted son of a bitch! I know exactly what you're doing standing there. You're not kidding anyone!" he screeched as he sped my way. "You're standing out here spying on my woman through the bathroom window while she's taking a shower!" he shouted at the top of his lungs as he pointed to the window not far from where I was standing. I didn't have the foggiest clue of what he was referring to, as I numbly stood there frozen in a mild state of shock, while preparing to defend myself physically if he decided to keep on charging in an effort to bowl me over.

Norman quickly exited the cruiser, heading my way, as Arnold stood in my face screaming, "I'm going to call the State Police on you and have you arrested for being a damned peeping Tom! You get the hell off my property, right now!" he angrily demanded.

Fortunately for me, Supervisor Nash and Inspector Downs had arrived at the scene just in the nick of time. Calmly, I said, "If you have a problem with my being here, sir, why don't you take it up with my boss who is right over there! You need to take it up with him, because I'm not moving from here!" I boldly stated. All the while, I was wondering if perhaps I wasn't in a heap of trouble.

There was no way in the hinges of hell I could have looked through the windows of this house watching a woman taking a shower, or watching anything else for that matter, even if I wanted to. Those windows hadn't been washed since the house was built decades ago—a real peeping Tom would need to have shattered the glass to get a peek inside! Besides, if the woman looked and acted anything like Arnold, I knew I wasn't missing anything.

Arnold quickly whirled around, with his arms flailing and screaming at the top of his lungs, as he headed toward Supervisor George Nash. "I want that sick son of a bitch arrested and removed from my property right now," he screamed to George, all the while he was pointing his shaking finger my way. "Your man is standing there, outside my bathroom window, watching my woman take a shower," Arnold yelled.

At this point during the conversation, I was about ready to run to the cruiser to finish off what warm milk Norman may have had left. My stomach was churning like never before. I was beginning to wonder if perhaps I wasn't getting an ulcer like my partner supposedly had.

George ever so calmly placed an arm around Arnold's shoulders and said, "Sir, if my young warden is doing what you say he is, we definitely will investigate it very thoroughly, and he'll be held accountable! I assure you!" With that being said,

Arnold seemingly calmed down and slowly regained his composure.

I felt my pulse rate increasing, as I wondered, "Holy cow! Am I being sold down the tubes, in order for Norman to get a little personal satisfaction for holding this notorious poacher accountable for his sins?" By now, I was about as comfortable as a swollen hemorrhoid sitting on a cold stump!

In the meantime, Norman led Arnold back to the cruiser, where he was questioning him about the illegal deer behind his house. George slowly strolled my way to take a look at the illegally shot critters tucked away in the hole in the ground.

With a big smirk on his face, George said, "Did you get a good and decent look at her, John?"

I saw absolutely no humor in his question, as I rather nervously tried to clear my good family name. "You look at those windows George! How to hell does he think anyone could be watching a woman taking a shower through them? You couldn't see through the dirt encased on those windows if you had X-ray vision for cripe sakes!" I nervously babbled.

"Don't worry about it, John. Calm down, calm down!" he muttered. "He's desperately searching for someone to shift his problems to. You're the perfect candidate! It's all a part of the game. As your career advances, you'll see bizarre incidents like this, time and time again." George was reassuring his hyper rookie warden. "People caught with their pants down and their hands in the cookie jar are always looking for a good excuse or an escape route, trying to divert the heat away from themselves and onto others. Today, you happened to have become that escape route! Don't worry about it!" he wisely stated.

His words of wisdom made me feel a little more at ease, until he grinned and once again inquired, "So, did you get a good look at her?" he chuckled. With the utmost respect for my boss's authority overriding that big mouth I was known to have, I never responded to his question. In my opinion, it didn't deserve a response!

Norman re-appeared, stating he'd obtained a full confession from Arnold, but Arnold wasn't about to implicate who had helped him in the midnight massacre. He was going to take full responsibility for the deer found on his property. With a confession in hand and no need to stay at the residence, we seized the four deer as evidence and struck out for the local crowbar hotel with Arnold, cuffed in the backseat.

On the way to jail, Arnold leaned forward within a few inches from my ear, "Well, Mr. Peeping Tom! According to your boss, it looks as though what little time I'm going to get in jail ain't gonna be nothing compared to what you'll be getting for spying on my woman! Who knows, maybe we'll even share a cell together," he deviously chuckled. I began searching frantically for Norman's milk jug! I definitely needed a drink, but it sure as hell would be something a little stronger than a swig of warm cow juice.

Arnold eventually plead guilty to the charges leveled against him. He was given a three-month jail sentence, along with a $750 fine.

Nothing more was ever said about the window-peeking rookie warden who provided him with a temporary excuse to divert attention away from his poaching activities. Although, there was an occasional inquiry from Supervisor George Nash, "Really John, was she a good looker?" he'd snicker, referring to that moment in time when I was indoctrinated into my very first poaching investigation. My adventure with Arnold, out in his backyard, would be one I'd never forget!

Where to, Sir?

Being out on patrol day and night, almost seven days a week, there were those times when certain things happened that we had absolutely no control over. Such was the case, one fall evening in 1978, when Norman arrived at my residence driving the new cruiser he'd received earlier that day. His new cruiser was equipped with the most modern up-to-date equipment the department had to offer.

It included everything from a new radio system, a new electronic siren, blue lights, and more—all of it workable from a panel of neatly arranged switches mounted on the dashboard. There was a switch allowing Norman to operate in stealth mode after dark. The switch cut out the brake lights and other forms of lighting in the car that might tip off a night hunter that we were quickly approaching their location. We could operate freely in the so-called stealth mode, driving along in the dark, utilizing the lights of the vehicle in front of us.

I had to admit, I was little jealous of my partner's new cruiser, especially after watching him bouncing all around it like a little kid who had just been given the greatest toy God ever created. I don't think I'd ever seen the old boy so excited! This cruiser was so elaborate that Norman even had an elaborate holder for that jug of warm cow juice he so desperately depended upon in times of crisis. Instead of ripping the car apart searching for that quick fix of his to cure that ulcer he claimed to have, now he knew right where it was whenever he needed it.

On this particular evening we were planning to work night hunters in my patrol area. It was still daylight, so we decided to sneak around the area, looking for a place to work later that night. But first we needed a quick bite to eat before heading out for the evening's surveillance.

Norman, proud of his new cruiser said, "You drive it, John. Tell me what you think. Besides, you know your area better than me. I just want you to see what a real cruiser is like," he sarcastically bragged, making sure I knew he had something a little better than mine! To be honest, had the shoe been on the other foot, I'd have done the same thing.

The department recently had converted all of our cruisers to a high-band radio system, with electronic sirens and a loud speaker to communicate with folks during searches or whenever a megaphone was needed. This new system required a separate microphone to be attached alongside the regular police mic on the dashboard of the cruiser. This was a story in itself, especially when trying to get old-timers like Norman used to speaking into the right microphone. More than once, the old boy grabbed the wrong microphone, and he couldn't understand why no one answered him.

I climbed in behind the wheel of Norman's shiny new machine, adjusted the seat to my satisfaction, and with my partner proudly perched beside me, we struck out for Ray's Diner in the nearby town of Knox, hoping to grab a quick bite before hunkering down for the night.

The country road to get to the busy little diner required traveling through a large area of local farm country. It was that time of the year when the farmers were doing their annual chores, and one of them was fertilizing their fields with fresh manure from their farms. The normal method used to spread the smelly fertilizer was a tractor hauling a manure spreader filled to the brim and overflowing with raw manure. The automatic spreader would toss the feces high into the air, covering a large area of the field they were spreading it in. To travel from the farms to the fields, they used the same narrow country roads as all the other traffic to reach their destinations. As they made their runs to and from the farm, large amounts of fresh, wet, smelly manure spilled from the overloaded spreaders onto the road, leaving quite a mess for other folks driving through the area.

Unfortunately, I turned onto one of these roads, and soon discovered it was covered with excess manure that had fallen off from these mechanical contraptions. There was no chance of avoiding it and I heard the wet dung splattering all over the side of Norman's shiny new cruiser.

"What the hell are you doing?" he screamed. He was bellowing loud enough to blow the excess wax out of my ears. "You're purposely driving through that shit and it's covering my car from one end to the other!" he angrily sputtered.

"I'm trying to miss it, Norman!" I yelled back, as if there was even the remotest chance of dodging it. But no amount of talking was about to convince my now grumpy partner that I hadn't done this on purpose.

"I knew it! I knew it! Letting you in behind the wheel of my new cruiser was just asking for disaster!" he screeched, as we continued along the narrow country road.

Adding to his obvious disgust, there was a sickening smell inside the vehicle as the raw manure splattered onto the car's manifold and baked itself to ashes. The odor it gave off wasn't any too appealing, to say the least.

Norman was as close to swatting me upside the head as he'd ever been. He was as grumpy as I'd ever seen the old boy and I could tell we were going to be in for a long and rough night. Little did I know that before the evening ended things were about to get worse, much worse!

As that sickening smell of burnt cow manure seeped in through the air vents of his new cruiser, I saw Norman retrieve that bottle of cow juice and give himself a much needed fix. By then he was pouting, the likes of which I'd never seen before.

"You're mad aren't you?" I pathetically inquired.

"You did that on purpose! I know you did, damn it all. I'll never get that smell out of the engine for as long as I've got this *#@ car!" he bitterly complained.

"Perhaps a little chow under his belt might sweeten him a little," I thought, as we pulled into the parking lot of Ray's Diner on Knox Ridge.

Once inside the restaurant, Norman seemed to have calmed down a bit. He was still highly irritated, but he wasn't alone. It seems that just about everybody inside the diner was griping about the mess of cow dung littering the area roads. We weren't the only ones finding ourselves caught up in the mess. Many of these disgruntled patrons were just as angry as Norman, which certainly helped my situation. Norman quickly joined in on their bitter cow dung conversations, while making it perfectly clear that he still felt that I'd driven through the manure on purpose. Of course those regulars in the diner who knew me well and could sense a little riff developing between the two of us, were quick to convince him that I'd more than likely done just that. A big help they were!

After chowing down on a light lunch, it was time to head out in search of a place to take up surveillance for the rest of the evening.

"Do you want your keys back?" I inquired, figuring surely that Norman would take over the operations from this point on.

"You might as well keep going, you can't do any more damage than what you've already done!" he sarcastically grunted. "Besides, it's your district and you know it better than I do, so you drive," he added.

Neither of us suspected that it could, and would, take yet another turn for the worse! Total darkness had settled in as we departed the diner. Norman appeared to be in a somewhat better mood than before. A short distance away, I decided to take the Abbott Road, a remote dirt road that wound its way out through the woods and into some rather large and remote fields. It was a place a night hunter just might venture by.

"Perhaps we can make a night working the fields down along this road, seeing as though I've received night hunting complaints there in the past," I suggested to my grumpy partner.

"It's your district. I'd just as soon get parked somewhere so I can open the window and get some fresh air in here, instead of smelling this shitty smell that you've managed to create!" he disgustedly grumbled.

We'd just started down the narrow dirt road and I was slowly poking along with the headlights bobbing up and down. Suddenly out of the woods charged a large buck with a huge rack. The damn fool had his head down and was coming straight at us. It all happened so quick there was no chance of avoiding a collision. The buck struck up against Norman's side of the car with a loud and rather sickening thud. The side mirror went scaling over the back of the car, as Norman watched the nose of the deer swipe across his side window.

I quickly brought the car to a screeching halt and a huge dust cloud encompassed the vehicle. I glanced back, just in time to see the deer jump up onto his feet and quickly disappear into the woods. His injuries were obviously minor, if any at all. Norman's cruiser however, wasn't so fortunate.

Norman immediately launched into a tirade of cuss words and phrases that no sane man would ever dare print! Let me explain it this way, Norman's Catholic priest certainly wouldn't have wanted to have been accompanying us on that fateful night. Because of his profanity-laced tirade, I expected Norman to be attending confessionals in the near future. He needed to clear his family name.

At least the old boy had managed to replenish his milk supply after we departed the restaurant, stopping at a nearby store. By now, he was guzzling the entire contents with sprays of milk flying everywhere.

Norman attempted to climb outside of his new cruiser in order to inspect the damage but he couldn't open the door. The buck had dented and wedged the passenger side door of his car, making the door inoperable. Norman was forced to crawl out through my side of the vehicle in order to investigate the damages.

It wasn't good. The large buck had totally destroyed the front fender and the side door of his new cruiser, the side mirror was gone, and there were large clumps of deer hair stuck onto the chrome siding that was peeled away from the side of the car.

"So *#@&** much for my having a brand new cruiser!" he screeched at the top of his lungs, with his arms flailing as if he was trying to take flight.

What else could I say? "Do you want to drive now?" I apologetically offered.

"No damn it, I don't! Let's see just what the hell else you can do to completely destroy my new car," he barked. "One damn thing for sure, I can't ride in the front seat," he grumbled, "so I'll crawl into the back seat and you'll just have to chauffeur me around!" he pathetically snickered.

I don't think he intended the dry comment to be anywhere near humorous. And that was the way the night ended, with Norman propped up in the back seat, hugging what was left of his bottle of warm milk, while sputtering to himself about how disastrous this evening's trip had been.

I restarted the car, fastened the seat belt, and peeking ever so cautiously over the back seat, I inquired, "Where to, sir?"

From the look I was getting back from the old coot, where he wanted me to go was not a place I cared to be!

Yet another great memory from the diaries. One that is just a little more humorous today than what it was on that fateful night.

Oops, I Forgot it Was There

I always wondered if my working partner ever got over that dreadful evening when I all but wrecked his new cruiser. Unintentionally, I might add! As time passed, Norm claimed he had forgotten the entire event and seemingly he was back to his old cheerful self. Still, there was a time or two, when we were in a conversation with others and he'd bring up that dreadful night and describe how I had entered his new cruiser into a demolition derby.

He managed to impress upon them that he was thoroughly convinced I had done it on purpose. But with time passing us by he claimed to have gotten over that horrific night. I still wasn't sure! I wasn't about to keep bringing up the subject. Although, I often found myself chuckling about it all!

Early in the evening of Oct. 6, 1979, Norman called my residence in a tizzy of sorts. Like so many times before, he was rather excited as he ordered me to meet him at his house just as soon as possible. He had received yet another anonymous tip— a hot complaint that required our immediate attention. Norman wouldn't share any of the specifics, making me wonder just what kind of a mess we'd be getting into as I sped for his Hartland mansion.

When I arrived at his house, he met me in the driveway with his red jacket and flashlight, carrying his usual jug of warm milk and a light snack. He obviously was in a big rush to get going without delay.

"What's up?" I inquired, sensing his urgency to not dilly-dally regarding this hot information he was responding to.

"We gotta head to Sugar Mountain in St. Albans," Norman sputtered. "I just got a telephone call from an anonymous informant that Sammy and his boys have just shot a large moose up on the mountain. Supposedly they are up there dressing it out right now," he stated.

"There's only one damn way of getting into that area—and there's only one way out, John boy. We can park at the end of the dirt road heading onto the mountain, and we've got 'em when they come out," he deviously snickered. "We might as well let them do all the dirty work of cutting up and quartering that critter. That way we won't be spending hours doing it ourselves," he sheepishly grinned.

If there was one thing about Norman, he was always thinking ahead. There was no doubt that Norman considered this to be a valid complaint. He knew the area, and he definitely knew the people involved.

As for me, I didn't have a clue of where Sugar Mountain was—for all I knew it could have been next to Mount Rushmore. I was simply flying low in my cruiser, following his instructions as to where to go. As I shot out over the narrow country roads at break-neck speeds, listening to his continuous bellowing about which turns to take next, I couldn't help but think back to that complaint a few years earlier, when we had responded to Arnold's house in Harmony to retrieve four illegally shot deer. I only hoped this wouldn't be a repeat performance.

"Those sons-of-guns," Norman yelled. "There's been a couple of bull moose up on that mountain for the past couple of years, and I knew damn well that it would only be a matter of time before Sammy and his boys couldn't resist the temptation of shooting them. I've been wanting to put my meat hooks into that crew for quite some time," Norman grunted. "Tonight's gonna be the night, John boy—tonight's gonna be the night!" he bragged.

I'd certainly heard the old boy use that phrase before!

Eventually we came to the end of the narrow dirt road leading onto Sugar Mountain. It was a desolate area, one with no houses or signs of civilization anywhere nearby.

Norman barked, "Back into that old field," as we slowly cruised along the rutted and gouged dirt road leading onto the mountain. "We'll wait right here until they come out, and then we'll jump them!" he schemed.

Doing as told, I automatically snapped the light switches off in my cruiser, making sure that none of my signal lights would be working, just in case I touched the brakes or hit the blinker lights giving away our presence. We were in the so-called stealth mode! Obviously, we didn't want anyone to know that we were in the area. Slowly I backed the Pontiac cruiser into the old grownup field adjacent to the rough and narrow mountain access road.

It was a cold and moonless night and stars twinkled brightly overhead. I shut off the engine and rolled down the windows and we patiently began the waiting game, listening and looking for any signs of activity in the woods beyond us. Norman was about as excited as I'd seen him in a long time. You'd have thought he was a young teenager on his first date by the way he was acting. He was fidgeting and swirling around in the front seat of my cruiser like a little puppy, confined in a small cage, anxiously waiting to be set free. The warm milk was dripping off his chin, as he constantly hoisted the milk jug up to his face, feeding his so-called ulcer.

As we sat in the still of night, listening to the traffic off in the distance and a pair of owls hooting nearby, Norman described the suspects he thought we'd be confronting.

"That damn Sammy and his boys. They've skated by for years," Norman sputtered. "I know damn well that most of last year they were night hunting out behind their place. I was told they were selling the meat to people in the Waterville and Skowhegan area. I bet right now they're thinking that with all this meat from a nice bull moose, it will bring them a small fortune. Well, I got news for them!"

As we patiently sat watching the road above us, we were suddenly startled by the glare of headlights bouncing off the trees, indicating a vehicle was coming toward us from the opposite direction. It was coming in from the highway, along the same route we'd taken to get into this God-forsaken place. This wasn't supposed to be happening!

"Jees-o, Jees-o, Jees-o," Norman stuttered. "They've got someone else coming in to help them," he theorized. "You've got to get this goddamn cruiser out of here right now or they'll spot us when they drive by. Quick," he screamed, "back up across the field and get your cruiser out of sight! I'll stay down here by the road and try to get their license plate number when they drive by."

I couldn't use my backup lights to see where I was going, otherwise I'd alert those folks coming our way that we were in the area.

"Is there anything out here in this old field I should be aware of?" I anxiously inquired, as I wasn't remotely familiar with the area. The last thing I wanted to do was to back into a tree or some other solid object.

"Nope, you're all set! It's just an old grownup field with a few small bushes, but nothing else. Hurry up and get to hell out of the way before they get here," he angrily barked. Norman had already jumped out of the car and was running toward the nearby ditch, hoping to get the license plate number of the vehicle as it passed by, in an effort to determine who else we might be dealing with.

I quickly shoved the car into reverse, shooting up across that old field just as fast and far as I dared to go, trusting my partner's advice that there was nothing to fear. That was my first mistake. The next thing I knew, I seemed to be floating in mid-air and in slow motion. Then there was a violent crash I came to a rather abrupt halt, right in among a patch of thick raspberry bushes. There I sat, staring straight up into the heavens, looking at the twinkling stars high up overhead. My head thumped hard against the head rest in the cruiser, followed by an eerie silence. I felt like I was strapped into a NASA rocket ready to be launched into outer space as I stared out through the windshield wondering what the hell had just happened.

Popping open my door, I found myself standing shoulder high in a patch of old raspberry bushes. There was a solid granite foundation holding up the front end of my cruiser. I'd backed squarely into an old cellar hole—one that either my partner didn't know existed, or he'd forgotten all about it. Maybe, just maybe, he'd forgotten on purpose!

Exiting the car, I fell into the prickly raspberry bushes as I cautiously climbed up out of the granite fortress which had swallowed up my cruiser. I heard Norman squealing down by the roadway in a fit of total hysteria. He knew I'd done something stupid. And I'd done it with no special thanks to him! I couldn't help but wonder if perhaps this wasn't his way to get a little personal payback for that time when I slowly wrecked his new cruiser.

At any rate, while I was floundering around in the cellar hole the incoming vehicle had already sailed on past us. Norman said it was a couple of coon hunters and their dogs. "Maybe they're using these coon dogs as an excuse to be in the area," he disgustedly fumed.

Then he chuckled," You're in that old cellar hole up there, aren't you? Oops, sorry, I forgot to tell you about it!" he sheepishly apologized.

We solicited a nearby woodcutter friend of Norman's into bringing his skidder into the area to pull my cruiser out from the cellar hole. This late-night savior, who so graciously offered his tow services, couldn't help chuckling to himself as he hooked his cables onto the front end of my cruiser and slowly yanked it back up onto solid ground. Other than a large dent in the front bumper, along with a few gouges and scrapes along the rocker panels, we were once again back in service.

As for Sammy and his boys, we ended up checking the same coon hunters when they came back down the mountain. They were people Norman was very familiar with, people who he claimed were as honest as the day is long. They'd been all over the mountain and hadn't seen anyone else up there. The original complaint was nothing more than a hoax. It appeared as if Sammy and the boys had been accused of doing something they hadn't. Or maybe it was Sammy and the boys who had sent us on a wild goose chase as they ventured elsewhere. It wouldn't have been the first time such a practice had been implemented!

The Sugar Mountain cellar hole incident certainly provided another fond memory for the diaries. That chaotic night wasn't just another normal night of patrolling by any means. It seemed as though there were no normal nights of patrolling anymore. Every evening was an adventure of its own, one with the element of surprise always lurking nearby. Perhaps that's why I enjoyed my job as much as I did. Constantly living and dealing with the unknown as a state of Maine game warden certainly was a good life! Who could ask for anything more?

Staying Awake

During the long fall hunting season, it was extremely difficult for us wardens to remain awake at night, especially after working from sunup to sundown for weeks on end, and then trying to stay alert when most normal folks were home, comfortably snuggled under the covers in their own warm beds. But we wardens knew this was the prime time to snag a poacher committing that cardinal sin of night hunting. No matter how hard one might try, when fatigue finally settled in, there was no means of resisting that opportunity to close the eyes and drift off into never-never land. Simply put, when the body could no longer fight total exhaustion, most of us experienced the natural reaction of going to sleep, whether we wanted to or not. Sometimes, we'd take turns napping for half an hour or so, sharing the rest period. But even then, when it was my turn to stay awake, when I heard my partner snoring on the other side of the cruiser, undoubtedly within minutes, I'd find myself joining him.

I recall one evening, or should I say early morning hour, when Norman and I were joined by Sgt. Bill Allen. All of us were sitting in the cruiser in the real wee hours of the morning, patiently watching the fields around us, hoping for that night-hunting activity that might venture our way. This particular area had been experiencing some early morning hunting, just prior to daylight, so we all decided to concentrate our efforts in hopes of bringing the illegal practice to an end.

I was operating the cruiser. We were chatting and talking among ourselves as the engine ran, keeping us nice and warm from the cold and frosty air. The talk consisted of the normal warden conversations: the current cases we were working on, some home or family issues we were trying to deal with, or the most famous topic of all, some sexual encounter of our own or others. Most of the sex talk was nothing more than stories of fascination and sweet dreams!

Before long the conversation inside the car had ceased. Bill was seated on the passenger side of my vehicle and Norman was stretched out on the backseat. They both were snoring away, completely oblivious to the big world around them. They sounded like a couple of operating chainsaws left running on idle. Their self-induced rest period left me with the duty of keeping that watchful eye out for any intruders venturing into the area. I was finding it extremely difficult to keep my own eyes open, but this particular area was too hot of a spot to pull up stakes and head home to the comforts of a warm bed. Determined to remain fully awake, as my companions continued snoozing away, I poured a hot cup of tea from my thermos jug and lit another cigarette to suck on. Between the two tasks, hopefully I'd be able to stay awake!

As I listened to the drone of the car's engine, and the snoring of my two compadres, I felt my eyes getting heavier and heavier, and I could feel my head starting to droop. Catching myself, I quickly straightened up and raised the cup of hot tea up to my mouth, slowly sipping at the contents, while puffing away on the lit cigarette. Between the two vices it seemed to be working and I kept a sharp eye out for any approaching car lights.

The next thing I knew, I was flopping around the inside of that cruiser screeching at the top of my lungs. Apparently I'd fallen asleep, dropping the entire cup of steaming hot tea and the lit cigarette directly in my lap. Bill then began trying to smash the windshield out of my cruiser, as he wildly flailed his arms after being so rudely awakened from that sound sleep he was so enjoying.

Poor Norman was picking himself up from the floorboards of the cruiser, and desperately searching for his milk jug to calm his now fragile nerves. He was sputtering and shouting some type of nonsense as he floundered around in the back seat. Most likely it was a profanity-laced barrage of comments aimed at me.

By then, I'd managed to flop outside the cruiser and into the cold and frosty night air, trying to cool off my crotch while snubbing out the smoldering flames in my pants, caused by the lit cigarette.

So much for fighting off the inevitable, we quickly decided it was time to call it a night. Rest assured, after a good day's sleep, we'd be right back at it again the next night.

Do You Solemnly Swear to Tell the Truth?

As I began my new career, one of the biggest fears I had was having to testify in court.

I can't fully explain why it was such a concern, other than knowing that someone could go to jail or pay a huge fine based totally on my testimony. This given authority was a little overwhelming to say the least. I had to be truthful no matter what, even though I knew the other side would use any tactics available to discredit my sworn testimony and show I had been wrong in bringing an action against their client. Through it all, I hoped to establish myself as being honest, credible, and fair to the courts and to the public I served.

Testifying in District Court wasn't bad, considering the fact that the only person judging my credibility would be the judge. In Superior Court, the legal process often calls for a jury of 12 peers selected from a pool of citizens from all over the county, some of whom I may have previously dealt with professionally or personally. My fear of testifying quickly disappeared once I accepted the fact that my testimony was nothing personal against those on trial; it was simply a matter of telling the truth and letting the chips fall wherever they may.

However, there were a few occasions when I found myself in some rather embarrassing situations while testifying. Some of these circumstances were brought about due to fatigue and frustration after working so many long hours. Others resulted from a casual remark or a downright stupid response on my part during a frustrating situation that arose during my case-building efforts. My language wasn't always commendable, to say the least. Let's put it this way, I wouldn't consider myself during those few times as being a good candidate for teaching Bible school—especially right after experiencing a run-in with some bozo who had just been in my face, screeching and screaming a volley of insults that included bad language and foul habits.

Throughout it all, my mother's words of wisdom always rang through, "True confessions are good for the soul." Certainly good advice from the matriarch of the family, who made damn sure I always was held accountable for my own actions at a younger age. No matter how horrid an event, or the circumstances surrounding it, the truth had to prevail in court to maintain my credibility and integrity within the legal system. A couple of embarrassing incidents come to mind—cases where I lost my professional cool at a time when my runaway mouth managed to put me in a rather compromising situation or two.

On Nov. 8, 1978, I happened upon a young hunter from the Winslow, Maine, area who was in possession of a loaded rifle while standing in the middle of a paved highway in Freedom, a direct violation of the hunting safety laws. This young man was no stranger to law enforcement. He'd spent more time sitting on the inside of a courtroom than most judges and was well known for a wide variety of criminal activities. Tim had a terrible attitude, one that was capable of "pissing off" the Pope and anyone around him. The very minute anyone of authority confronted Tim, he would turn defiant and obstinate.

Upon determining that his rifle was loaded, I calmly advised him I was going to issue a summons for the violation. As expected, the discussion quickly went downhill for what seemed like a 15-minute, out-of-control tirade by the little twerp. I politely asked him for his hunting license, which brought another typical Tim response; "I ain't got no gawdamn license and now I suppose you're going to write me up for that too, you *#** pig!"

As calmly as I possibly could, I said, "No Tim, I'm not. I've no intentions of giving you a summons at this point. Instead, I'm placing you under arrest. We're going to the county jail. I'm all done putting up with your disrespectful crap today!"

With that, I placed him in handcuffs and away we went, headed for the crowbar hotel in Belfast. Tim continued running his mouth right straight ahead along the way. Listening to his constant insults was enough to try the patience of any sane man. But I simply drove along paying him no attention.

A short distance later Tim said, "You think you're so *%$*# smart. I do have a hunting license, you #^$!# jerk, and it's right here in my back pocket!" he smartly screamed.

By now I was furious. Defiantly I glanced over at Tim and said, "At this point in time Tim, I don't really give a damn what you have. You said you didn't have one back there, you flatly refused to produce it, so now you can take that license that you claim to have suddenly found and stick it up your arse, as far as I'm concerned. You had your chance to be civil and you blew it!" I screamed.

"We'll see," he mouthed back. "I'll see you in court, you *#*% - *** hole!" he shouted.

Personally, I wanted to reach over and bat him upside the head. The miserable little creep knew just how to push the right buttons to incite bitterness during any contact he had with the authorities, and I knew better than to bite. Truthfully speaking, probably that's what he was hoping for. Then he could sue me, while making a little money off his own self-righteous indignation. He'd certainly been there before! In the past, Tim had made the rounds with just about every cop south of Bangor and north of Augusta. Whenever he was confronted, it ended up in the same old mouth and pony show, with Tim getting a free ride to jail. I think he thrived on making the trip.

Tim decided to have a jury trial in Superior Court regarding our little fall confrontation. I figured this would be an easy case, with little leeway for a defense attorney to argue, but then I should have known better. There never was such a thing as an easy case! I testified to the circumstances of the incident under questioning from then-District Attorney William Anderson. It appeared to be a cut-and-dried matter until the court-appointed attorney for Tim began his examination.

"Warden Ford, isn't it true that my client actually had a hunting license? And isn't it true that he attempted to show you his license on the way to jail," he bluntly inquired.

Suddenly I could feel my buns tightening and a dryness in my throat as I began testifying, "When I asked him for his license, he arrogantly stated he didn't have one. This happened prior to my arresting him for the loaded gun incident," I humbly squawked. "As a matter of fact, he wouldn't produce any identification," I bravely stated, hoping that my quick answer would suffice.

"But Warden Ford, didn't my client want to show you that license on the way to jail? And do you recall exactly what you told him he could do with that license?" the defense attorney inquired. I couldn't help but notice that smirk on his face. It was that kind of an "I gotcha!" moment! "Uh, oh, here we go!" I thought. Without a doubt it was a little more bun-sucking time in the witness chair, as I'm sure my face turned a beet red color.

I could see that puzzled look on the district attorney's face, as he now wondered what I was about to testify to. Obviously, it was something I'd either purposely forgotten to forewarn him about, or I didn't dare warn him about, hoping that the issue wouldn't come up during the trial. The silence in the courtroom was eerie. I swallowed hard and my mouth suddenly went dry, real dry.

Boldly, I glanced over at the 12 jurors seated close by and said, "Yes sir, I remember exactly what I told him! I told him that he could take his license and stick it up his arse!"

The outburst of uncontrollable laughter from the jury was almost deafening. Even the judge had a hard time trying to maintain his composure. The only ones in that courtroom who were not even close to smiling were poor Bill, the district attorney, and myself. If looks could have killed, I'd have been dead on the spot for failing to mention this little fact to our prosecutor. Deservedly so, I might add.

It was a humiliating lesson to be sure. The jury was in deliberations for a short five minutes before coming to a quick decision. I lost the hunting without a license charge on Tim. With this horrible experience behind me, one would've thought I'd have learned a valuable lesson. But sometimes a person has to be stung by the bees twice or more before they finally get the message.

A similar incident happened a few weeks later when Warden Norman Gilbert and I were called to a night hunting complaint in the town of Winterport. The complainant observed a van driving into a nearby field late in the evening, then heard a couple of rifle shots. He was quite confident they'd shot one of several grazing deer. The complainant was able to obtain the license plate number from the vehicle as it quickly sped out of the field and flew past his house.

Norman and I immediately headed for the area, hoping to catch the culprits before they could leave, but before we got there, a sheriff's deputy went barreling into the region to check on the complaint himself, and had scared the perpetrators away, or so we thought. It was unknown if these poachers had bagged a deer or not. Needless to say, Norm and I were highly disgruntled with the entire effort. The deputy, while responding with good intentions, more than likely had ruined any chances of us catching these folks with the goods. Upon our arrival into the area, we both concluded that more than likely our response would be nonproductive.

A check of the vehicle's registration revealed the van was owned by a young man who lived close by—a man I'll call Harry (not his real name). We immediately headed to Harry's house where sure enough the van was parked in the driveway. No one appeared to be around. There was a stream of fresh water running down the driveway, indicating that the inside of the van had just been washed—certainly washing a vehicle at this late hour of the night was not a common practice for anyone. I noticed the lights were on inside the residence, but no one came outside to greet us. Knocking on the door, it appeared as though no one was home.

As I walked around the van I observed a trail of deer hair and blood leading out behind the garage and into the nearby woods. Following the drag marks, and the deer hair and blood, I found a freshly killed deer hanging from a nearby tree out behind the garage. Norman and I quickly confiscated the critter, dragging it back to the cruiser. As we were hoisting the animal into the trunk, Norman noticed a young man was peeking out through the kitchen window, watching our every move.

Completely frustrated by the series of events thus far, I made a mad dash back to the residence and pounded loudly upon the door. I could see Harry peeking at me from inside the house, but he wouldn't come to the door.

Disgustedly, I shouted, "Harry, if you don't open this blankety-blank door I'm going to kick it to *%$* open and come in there after you." Certainly this was not an approach I was used to making, and one which had allowed my frustrations of the evening to show.

Rather sheepishly, Harry responded to my request. There was fresh blood and deer hair on his boots, which gave me the probable cause to make an arrest for possession of a deer killed at night and out-of-season. After all of the events we thought had gone wrong in our investigation that night, now it appeared to be an open and closed case.

What had begun as a real fiasco somehow turned into a rather productive evening after all—until the day of the trial in District Court before Judge Jack Smith.

Harry solicited a local attorney who questioned me at length regarding the events of that evening. Everything seemed to be going quite well until the defense attorney calmly inquired if I recalled the manner in which I'd approached Harry, as he was safely inside the sanctuary of his own house. I suddenly felt my buns sticking to the witness chair, hoping beyond hope that I wouldn't have to repeat, word for word, the shameful demand I'd made upon Harry in order to get him to open the door. But the defense attorney insisted, "Now, Warden Ford, would you mind telling this court your exact words as you angrily demanded my client to open the door of his own home, in the middle of the night, as he simply pondered who could be intruding onto his property at such a late hour."

A hushed silence suddenly befell the courtroom as I nervously squirmed in the witness chair. It was a classic Perry Mason moment for sure. I knew I had to repeat my comments exactly the way it went down, or the relentless hounding by the defense attorney would refresh my memory. It certainly was not a proud moment in my young career by any means. But I knew it would be better coming from me now, rather than having that line of testimony drag on endlessly and word by word be disclosed.

Slowly, I cleared my throat, waiting for my heart to stop racing. By then, the judge was leaning forward on the bench and the crowded courtroom was as quiet as a morgue. All of their eyes were focused my way, as this anticipated testimony by the defense attorney was a deciding moment of the trial.

"Yes sir," I slowly mumbled, "I told Harry if he didn't open that *&$*# door, I was going to kick it off the hinges and come to hell in there after him!" My face had to have been as red as a freshly picked tomato, as the courtroom erupted in total hysteria. Like a time or two before, I noticed that even the judge had suddenly leaned back in his chair with a silly smirk on his face.

The defense attorney, quite confident that I'd never accurately tell my version of the events, simply grinned as to my obvious moment of sheer discomfort. He quickly rested his case after pointing out to the judge, "Poor Harry was in fear for his own safety, your honor, especially with a madman making such uncalled for demands at the door of his home during the wee hours of the night." By far, this was not one of my prouder moments in the courtroom, but it was a good lesson learned, or so I thought.

Judge Smith exonerated Harry of the charges against him. However he was quick to inform Harry that it wasn't my lack of professionalism that led him to his decision, but instead he felt the wardens should have obtained a search warrant before seizing the deer. His ruling on this case was strictly a curtilage issue (*area subject to search and seizure*) and had nothing to do with my unprofessional approach toward the defendant. Harry was free to go!

I met the judge in the hallway shortly after the trial. Sporting a big smile he said, "That was quite a day we had in the courtroom today, huh, John? Did you kind of lose your professional cool on that one? I admire you, though, for telling the truth. That was obviously a rather difficult moment for you, but we are all human. Sometimes, we have those kinds of days."

There would be more lessons in courtroom testimony in the future, but none as egregious as these two had been. They definitely were a couple of good lessons learned the hard way.

The story with Harry however didn't end with that trial. Within a few weeks we had yet another confrontation. At that time I found the incident to be a bit disconcerting. It was obviously a little payback for my intrusion into his house in the middle of the night. But in time I actually found myself laughing at the courage of Harry and his cronies, even if their actions were highly motivated by a little "Budweiser power!"

You Little Stinker, You!

Jan. 16, 1979, was my normal day off from patrolling in the wilderness. The unusually warm temperatures that evening had left the countryside encased in a layer of dense fog.

Due to the heavy layer of fog, I was quite content right at home, enjoying a little quality time with Little John and Mrs. Ford, not worrying about driving around in the sloppy and miserable conditions outside. Besides, what possibly could be going on in the outside world on such a foggy and miserable night?

As I sat comfortably in my living room chair watching the television, I noticed headlights slowly coming into the driveway. I wondered, "Who to hell could this be, out poking around on such a foggy night?" I leaned forward staring out the window, hoping to get a glimpse of who it was. I barely could see the vehicle through the thick fog, as the car drove closer to my garage door. After a quick beep of the horn, I observed a rather large object scaling up over the vehicle, landing on the ground directly in front of the garage doors. Then the vehicle slowly backed around in my driveway and proceeded toward town.

Mrs. Ford said, "Who to heck was that?"

"I dunno," I sputtered, "but whoever it was just threw something in front of the garage door and now they're leaving. I'm going out to see what it is, and try to catch up with them," I shouted as I scrambled out of the house wearing only my dungarees, slippers, and a T-shirt—hardly what anybody would consider to be a proper uniform.

I quickly jumped into the cruiser after locating a large dead skunk that had been tossed in front of my garage door. "Somebody obviously was sending a personal message in a ballsy kind of way," I disgustedly thought.

I shot out of the driveway, catching up with the vehicle a short distance away. I observed four young men in the car as I snapped the blue lights on, signaling for them to stop. As calmly as I could under the circumstances, I hustled up to the driver's side of the vehicle.

"Good evening sir, I need to see your driver's license and registration," I politely demanded, as I flashed the light into the vehicle to observe who was inside.

The four young men were obviously in a celebratory mood as evidenced by the number of beer bottles rolling around on the floor and piled alongside of them. They watched my every move as I asked the driver to come back to my vehicle. Not one of them spoke a word.

I recognized one of the culprits involved as Harry. It was Harry, whom I'd lost my cool with earlier that fall and threatened to kick his #*%#* door down and march to hell in there after him if he didn't open it up, as he cowardly hid behind the kitchen walls. More than likely it was Harry who had thrown the dead skunk into my driveway. If Harry wasn't the tosser, he sure as hell conned his drunken comrades into committing the act. One thing for sure, they weren't about to say who the wild skunk tosser was.

Harry's buddy Gary calmly sat in my cruiser, refusing to identify the skunk-tossing culprit. Instead, he nervously chuckled about the bravery of the whole event. "It must have fallen off my grill," he snickered. By law, Gary being the operator of the vehicle, was responsible for the actions of his passengers, so I arrested him for littering, rather than letting them simply drive away from the area thinking they'd pulled the wool over my eyes.

Needless to say, my temperament wasn't the best—far from it to be exact! Not knowing what kind of a fiasco I was getting into as I began my pursuit, I notified the Maine State Police of my circumstances and informed them that I was pulling over a vehicle a short distance from the house. One never knew what kind of a mess they could find themselves in, so it was nice to know help was on the way. Upon hearing the radio traffic, Maine State Police trooper Rexford Kelley quickly came to my assistance.

Rex was another trooper buddy I enjoyed patrolling with. We constantly played practical jokes on each other whenever the opportunity arose. Although Rex wasn't fond of jokes aimed his way, he sure liked to play them on others. His easy irritability and a slight lack of good-natured humor for a prank played upon him made it all the more challenging and entertaining for those of us who were looking for a laugh or two at Rex's expense! Admittedly, I'd pulled more than my fair share of pranks against my buddy with the blue uniform. So I reckon it was only appropriate that Rex responded to my situation on this night. In other words, Rex appeared to be rather jubilant that these little hoodlums had actually played a devious prank on, of all people, me, and that my sense of humor was seriously lacking this time around! Maybe Rex was right, but the jury was still out.

I arrested Gary for the littering offense, holding him accountable for the actions of his cronies. Rex offered to transport Gary to jail, saving me the trip. We advised his buddies where they could go to bail him out. Like they didn't know!

I still envision that satisfied and rather silly smirk on Rex's face as he headed off toward the crowbar hotel, chuckling over the entire fiasco. I'd like to have been a fly on the wall as Rex and Gary headed for the slammer. But then, on second thought, maybe I wouldn't. The rest of the crew was issued a stern warning to stay away from my property, or the next time the consequences could, and would, be much more severe.

In reality this little harmless incident was a comical situation, although a bit humiliating at the time. Those young men involved really were good old boys, just out sharing a few beers and boldly sending a message to that damned old woods cop who had harassed one of them a few weeks earlier.

This wasn't the first time I had a subtle message sent my way by those who felt threatened by my profession. In the past I'd found deer heads and hides thrown in my door yard in Burnham, rabbits stuffed in my mailbox, and even a stolen two-hole outhouse blocking the end of my driveway one morning. So this was just one more incident to be added to the diaries of pranks played upon the lawmen in the area. In most of those cases, however, I never got to know who had committed the dastardly deeds. But in this situation, I got to witness it as it happened—a rarity, to say the least.

I wasn't alone in receiving a form of retaliation from some of my former clientele. My trooper buddy Rex and his partner

Richard Golden experienced a more serious situation one day while they were eating lunch at a Belfast restaurant. As they were inside snacking on a midday meal, a couple of hoodlums with whom they'd dealt with in the past were outside slashing all eight tires on their cruisers. That incident was far more serious and destructive than anything I'd experienced, especially since it endangered the safety and welfare of the entire area. If an emergency had arisen that required an immediate response, neither of these two troopers could have gone. Eventually Rex apprehended the hoodlums involved, bringing them to justice at a later time.

So in essence, as time passed I considered the skunk-tossing incident as simply a hazard of the profession. A stinking one at that! This little skunk caper caused no harm and really was comical once I was able to put it all into perspective.

As in Harry's case, when he was found not guilty because of a legal technicality, Gary too was found not guilty on a technicality when he appeared before the same Judge Smith a few days later. His case was dismissed without prejudice, due to a recent change in the littering laws. Two weeks earlier, littering had been classified as a civil infraction and was no longer an arrestable offense. Unfortunately, we officers had yet to have been apprised of the new law. So Gary, like his buddy Harry, other than being inconvenienced for their time appearing before the judge, received no punishment for his actions. I was beginning to wonder just who to hell "the little stinker" really was—myself, Harry, Gary, or that damned old judge who I was contemplating calling a name or two of my own.

Oh well, in the end it made for more pleasant memories for the diaries, and I still find myself chuckling today at those events from the past. One thing for sure, life was never dull in the great profession I'd chosen.

One Mile of Despised Real Estate

The little cub was lying in the breakdown lane.

My assigned patrol area consisted of a one-mile stretch of nothing but paved highway in Burnham that was located along the I-95 corridor between the towns of Pittsfield and Clinton. The only way for me to access it was to drive to Clinton and head north, or to travel to Pittsfield and go south. No matter which route of travel I took, it was a long damn way to go. I despised the journey on every complaint I was sent to on that lonely one-mile stretch of highway. Whenever something happened out there requiring my services, it seemed to always occur at the most inopportune time. Getting there was a pain in the rump. I'd find myself driving all around Robin Hood's barn to reach the area. There was nothing but speeding cars and thick woods. No houses, no people, no nothing except a steady stream of travelers, all of them racing from one part of the state to the other. Other than an occasional night hunter who scanned the green and grassy shoulders adjacent to the pavement, searching for the glassy eyes of a grazing buck, I had few worries about poaching along this miserable stretch of pavement.

Most of the complaints within this mile of nothingness, included countless vehicle collisions with deer and other wild critters. All of them demanding an immediate trip to clean up the mess and to make out the necessary paperwork for some poor traveler who had the misfortune of colliding with one of these beasts. Without fail, those folks bitterly complained about the long wait they had before I arrived on scene. As I dealt with a cranky complainant while parked along the breakdown lane, I determined that nothing short of an army tank blocking the entire highway would ever get those motorists flying through the area to slow down. They'd gawk at what was happening and wonder why my blue emergency lights were flashing, while cruising past us like speeding bullets looking for a place to land.

I desperately tried pawning off this hated section of highway to my working partner, Norman Gilbert. But he wasn't in the mood for purchasing any more real estate. Matter of fact, when I first assumed my duties as a rookie warden, I later learned how the old coot had pawned off more than a third of his district to me at the time, and I was none the wiser that I'd been duped. Of course, back then, being young and enthusiastic, and he with more than 20 years of service, I was more than willing to accept more responsibility and he damn well knew it. He took full advantage of my enthusiasm. Foolish, foolish me!

A couple of incidents along that desolate patch of pavement made it into the diaries. One of them occurred on April 14, 1981, when I received an urgent call from the Maine State Police requesting that I head that way after a motorist reported a bald eagle had been struck on the busy interstate highway. Supposedly, the eagle was sprawled out in the middle of the road, causing quite a commotion from those folks flying by the dead bird at warp-factor-eight. After all, not one of these morons could be bothered to stop and remove our national bird from the tarred highway. At that time, eagles were extremely rare in our state. As such, they were at the top of the nation's most endangered species list. The very chances of seeing an eagle in the wild was like hoping to see the abominable snowman in the middle of a blizzard, snowshoeing across the trails of Frye Mountain in Montville.

When I received the complaint from the Maine State Police, I was busy preparing for a speaking engagement scheduled for later that evening in the city of Belfast, some 40 miles away. Time-wise, I was pushing the clock, driving all the way to Pittsfield, getting on the southbound lane, heading south, while looking for an injured eagle. But duty called and I had to respond. Needless to say, I wasn't letting any grass grow beneath my feet as I quickly headed that way. Entering the highway in Pittsfield, I immediately drove south to where the eagle was supposedly located. In the meantime, the police dispatchers had received several more reports of the bird on the highway and they were inquiring as to my estimated time of arrival. Disgustedly, I advised them I was going as fast as I could.

Off in the distance, I observed a large bird sprawled out in the breakdown lane, apparently the object of my search. Initiating the emergency blue lights of my cruiser, warning those unconcerned motorists of my presence, I slowly pulled into the breakdown lane and up to where the motionless carcass lay splattered on the pavement. As I headed for the carcass, I thought, "What the hell am I going to do with an injured eagle? I'm going to barely have enough time to make it to the speaking engagement in Belfast as it is." These folks had planned and advertised my presence at this public forum for quite some time. I'd be hard pressed trying to justify to them of how I was on the interstate rounding up an injured bird of prey.

As it turned out, I didn't have to worry about what to do with the eagle. There wasn't one! Instead, I found a damned old chicken that had obviously died from injuries it received while trying to cross the busy speedway. Wherever it came from was anyone's guess! I checked with the dispatcher to see if I was in the right location.

"10-4" the dispatcher stated. "You're at the right place!"

I felt my jaw tighten, as I disgustedly stated, "Augusta, there's NO eagle here. There's a dead chicken and that's it! A far cry from an eagle!"

Rather humbly, the dispatcher replied, "10-4. The reports we received said it was an eagle. Sorry, John!"

"Sorry my a$*," I thought to myself.

I could tell from the tone of the dispatcher's voice that they all were getting quite a kick out of my wasted adventure down there in police headquarters. Immediately, several buddy officers who were apparently listening to the radio traffic, started mimicking the sounds of a flock of chickens, "Buawk, buawk – buawk – buawk – buawk!" There's nothing like adding a little fuel to the fire. My disposition was not what you might have considered as jovial at that particular moment. I can't tell you how badly I wanted to pick up that microphone and say something really devious to the twerps listening on the other end, but I thought better of it.

I quickly removed the dead fowl from the roadway and sped toward Clinton, heading straight for Belfast and hoping the audience I was scheduled to speak before would understand why I wasn't there on time. That damn stretch of disgusting real estate left bad memories every time I went there.

The one call that I remember the most from out there in nowhere land, was received in the middle of the night. A young black bear cub had been killed along this desolate "highway to hell." The last thing I wanted to do was to crawl out of bed in the middle of the night to retrieve a dead bear cub lying in the middle of I-95. But duty once again called and away I went.

It was another long ride to Pittsfield to enter the heavily traveled highway, where I found myself cruising along the southbound lane at warp speed. I admit, I was flying low, half-baked for having to get up at such a horrible hour and having to respond to such a complaint. After all, the damn thing was dead. Obviously it wasn't going anywhere.

As I sped along, I kept one eye peeled to the breakdown lane, searching for the small bear carcass. Spotting a dead bear cub in the middle of the breakdown lane at 2 a.m. while cruising along at 70-plus mph was no easy task. But suddenly there it was, halfway between the breakdown lane and the travel lane. I damn near clipped the little cub carcass as I started my descent, hoping to land within a reasonable distance of the poor critter. By the time I skidded to a complete stop, I found myself quite a distance away from the young bear. Rather than backing up, possibly causing a collision, I initiated the emergency flashers on my cruiser and slowly struck out on foot, hiking up the side of the road to where the tiny black corpse was lying. I admit, he was a cute and cuddly little fellow. But sadly, he was no match for the mechanical monster that had run him down. I quickly grabbed his hind feet and began the long and rather slow trek back to my cruiser.

Suddenly, fairly close by, I heard a lot of crashing and banging out in the woods, noises that seemed to be headed my way. Only then did the thought cross my feeble mind that perhaps momma bear might be watching as I carted her youngster away by his hind legs and that maybe, just maybe, she might be coming to his defense. Did I mention that my cruiser was quite some distance away? I suddenly found myself picking up and lowering my clodhoppers at a clip that would have made any Olympian proud. As I scurried back toward the security of my own mechanical monster idling off in the distance, I was setting yet another one of those record 100-yard dashes that I found myself recording into the diaries over the years.

Fortunately, whatever had been thrashing nearby was no longer making any noise. But perhaps it was due to the fact that I was causing quite a commotion myself. I was high-tailing it along the breakdown lane at nearly the same speed as the cars on the paved drag strip. I'm sure my presence, trotting along the highway like a racehorse on a dirt track, carrying a bear cub in my hand, must have been quite a sight for the 2 a.m. travelers passing by.

Yup, there was something about that damned miserable one mile stretch of pavement that I detested. As if getting to it wasn't bad enough, it seemed as if every time I went there, something weird or unusual happened. And, as I stated before, never do I recall an incident occurring on that hated mile of roadway when I wasn't already busy somewhere else within my district.

That's the way it was in the world of law enforcement. We didn't get to pick and choose where to patrol, or the incidents we'd rather spend our time working on. The duties of a game warden came with the good, the bad, and at times, the damn right disgusting. I-95 proved to be one of those disgusting places. I guess that's why I liked the job so much. Anticipating the unknown was a reality every morning when I settled into my cruiser for another day at the job.

I was well aware that before my career ended, I'd again find myself headed to Pittsfield or Clinton, making that journey to the most despised stretch of highway in my patrol area. Even today, after retiring so many moons ago, I still find myself cussing that one-mile stretch of pavement whenever I'm out on the I-95 corridor.

Talk about the I-95 corridor. Read on!

A Forced Eviction

The young moose took up residency in the median strip of I-95.

In 1980, Maine had authorized its first moose hunt in several years. The event was to be held later that fall. Ironically, on May 26, 1980, a young cow moose decided to claim its residency in a rather dangerous location. She set up housekeeping between the northbound and southbound lanes of Maine's busiest highway, on Interstate 95 in the town of Palmyra.

The very thought of a moose playing in traffic along Maine's busiest superhighway was a threat not only to society, but to the welfare of the animal. After all, a moose colliding with a vehicle traveling in excess of 70 mph could be fatal for all involved. Year after year, state statistics recorded more than one unsuspecting driver crashing into one of these huge creatures. Every one of them ended with catastrophic results. Unlike a deer, which is much smaller and has yellow eyes that reflect when headlights of an approaching automobile shine on them, a moose gives no such warning after dark. The eyes of a moose do not shine like those of a deer. A driver can be clipping along at a normal rate of speed, when suddenly right before him is a dark form representing a beast weighing 1,000 pounds or more. The force of the collision causes the long-legged moose to be catapulted into the air. Usually the large carcass is driven through the windshield of the vehicle, while peeling back the vehicle's roof in the process. God pity anyone beneath it! Seldom are the injuries minor to the passengers. Matter of fact, in most cases, the injuries are usually quite severe, if not fatal.

This particular young moose did not seem to be displaying the normal symptoms of moose sickness. Moose sickness is caused by a parasitic worm known as the meningeal worm. It is passed along to moose from deer in their shared grazing areas. The worm eventually works its way through the blood stream and into the brain of the animal. There is no known cure for the disease with moose. Deer, for some strange reason, do not experience the same fatalistic characteristics caused by this dreaded parasite. An infected moose can be found wandering aimlessly around in circles, incapable of defending itself after having lost all fear of predators or dangers, such as a man or moving vehicles.

And so, May, 26, 1980, several of us were dispatched to the busy interstate in an attempt to drive this stubborn moose out and away from the median strip where it had taken up residency. The young cow, weighing between 500 and 600 pounds, was not very cooperative. She wasn't about to be forcefully evicted from her new home. Extreme caution had to be taken, making sure we didn't drive the critter from the narrow strip of woods separating the four lanes of busy highway, directly into the path of the oncoming traffic—traffic which was flying through the area about as uncontrollable as the moose was, in between the two lanes.

There's something about a few of those interstate drivers that really baffles me. Trying to get them to slow down for their own safety, was about like sending a severe sex addict into a house of ill repute only to watch TV and not expecting him to partake of any additional activity. First, there were those drivers who flatly refused the signal to slow down, thinking it was their God-given right to clip along the smoothly paved highway at a speed equivalent to that of a NASCAR driver racing in the Daytona 500. These operators seemed to have the impression that while they're on the superhighway, nothing can prevent them from going as fast as they want to. No amount of hand signals, blue lights, road blockages or barriers, caused them to slow down to a speed that might protect them from impending danger. I actually had my own little private hand signal that I wanted to use, but I thought better of it. I knew if I were to lose control and flip it the wrong way, the bosses wouldn't be very happy.

Secondly, there were those curious individuals who insisted on stopping along the busy highway to witness the ongoing event firsthand, causing even more chaos in an already chaotic situation. Most of these folks barely parked off the travel portion of the busy highway. They quickly exited their cars in order to get a good view of the contingency of wardens trying to herd a moose back into the woods where it belonged. Advising them to move along usually resulted in a wrinkled-up nose and a little hand signal of their own.

Lastly, the moose itself posed the biggest problem. None of us could predict where the beast would go and when. The eviction process being implemented upon Ms. Bullwinkle on this day was definitely a fly-by-the-seat-of-your-pants and hope-for-the-best type of operation. We were aided by several wardens, biologists and state troopers. They parked their vehicles, with their emergency blue lights flashing, in both the northbound and southbound lanes. Officers stood along the edge of the highway near the median strip as the forceful eviction of the moose was conducted.

Herding this moose out of the small patch of woods and off into the big pasture was quite a challenge indeed. The first attempt was going quite well until some moron driving a huge tractor-trailer rig flew through the area at warp-factor-eight, blowing his horn the entire way and forcing the moose to flee back into the same area from where she had been driven. Needless to say, the eviction of Ms. Bullwinkle wasn't going very well.

As I recall, the state police officers who attempted to get this trucker to slow down as he approached them at a high rate of speed in the passing lane, used that same hand signal I'd contemplated using a little earlier—especially after he cruised through the area at 70 plus mph, laying on the horn, grinning from ear to ear, and ignoring their demands to slow down. This sudden show of professional disrespect from my brother officers toward the Peterbuilt monster and its driver, brought a devilish little smirk to my face. I heard them loudly cussing out the guy after he ignored their signals to slow down. Better them than me, I figured. In an act of sheer frustration, I'd probably have contemplated placing a few rounds next to his window, had I been the officer standing out by the road. Figuratively speaking, that is!

On our second attempt at the eviction process, we finally managed to drive Ms. Bullwinkle from the median strip and into the heavy patch of woods on the north side of the interstate, where she quickly sauntered away from the busy highway. Concluding our mission was successful and that a possible tragedy had been averted, we all departed the area quite proud of our day's accomplishments.

But by mid-afternoon the next day, we were once again dispatched to the same location. It seems our unwanted tenant decided she wasn't about to be evicted from her home by a gang of damned old game wardens, biologists, and state troopers. She decided to return to the little thicket in the median strip in a total defiance of the order of law. Maybe in her own independent way, she was protesting our state legislature for authorizing a moose hunt in the first place.

This time around, our eviction attempt definitely required a much more drastic action before someone was hurt or killed. The department biologists arrived with a trusty dart gun, purposely designed for emergencies such as this.

Once again, the efforts to control the speeders were about the same as the day before. Tempers were flaring as travelers seemed to ignore the safety precautions to slow them down. Finally, after a bit of moose-herding, almost as if it were a round-up at a rodeo, two drug-filled darts were successfully planted directly into Ms. Bullwinkle's rump.

Now the problem was, when would the drugs take effect, and where would the moose go in the meantime? The last thing we needed was to have her stagger into the middle of the passing lane and collapse. Hell, there would be no end to the carnage that would ensue if that were to occur. One thing was for sure, Lady Bullwinkle wouldn't be afraid of any approaching vehicles once the drugs took effect. And if the oncoming vehicles continued to refuse to slow down, we just might end up witnessing one hell of a collision.

As the drugged moose staggered through the median, several of us followed along a short ways behind her, waiting for that moment when she would finally collapse under the influence of the drugs. Fortunately, we were able to contain the critter well within the median strip, even after a few hectic moments of scaring her away from the highway. In what seemed like an eternity, she finally collapsed in a comatose trance in the ditch. She was ready to be transported away from the major highway and into an area she could claim as home. It took several of us to lift the large creature into the back of the biologist's truck, where we held her head up in a normal position to keep her airway open, preventing her from suffocating.

Lady Bullwinkle was transported to a remote area of Canaan, where she was unloaded and monitored until the drugs began to wear off. In the end, she slowly came around. Standing up on her feet, she slowly trotted off into the wilderness, staggering all the way, like a drunk with a bad hang-over.

Two days of riding herd and driving moose along the interstate was quite enough excitement for this old boy. I was sure there would be a car-moose collision before this caper was over. I still find myself in total disbelief regarding those citizens who simply assumed that driving at a high rate of speed on the interstate is their God-given right, as they completely ignore any attempts of trying to get them to slow down. I bet there's a host of state troopers who would agree with my assessment, especially seeing as though they have to deal with drivers' hair-raising issues on a daily basis. I could see why they shake their heads in total disbelief at some of these accident scenes and other wild scenarios they confront on the paved drag strip. Would I want to patrol that paved race track on a daily basis? No thanks! I was quite happy to have a profession where I could stick to patrolling the woods, lakes, and streams, and to hell with the paved highway!

This entire two-day event created yet another one of those memorable moments for the diaries. The eviction of Ms. Bullwinkle had been satisfactorily completed, without anyone being seriously injured. That in itself was good.

Whitetail Memories

The almighty whitetail deer certainly provided several entertaining and memorable moments during my career. "Old Whitetail," as he is called, definitely is one of the most sought-after big game animals in our state.

God only knows what there is about standing a big old buck, sporting a huge set of antlers, in front of a man with a high-powered rifle that entices him into doing some of the damnedest things imaginable. It appears as though the bigger the rack of antlers, the more unpredictable the hunter becomes in order to satisfy his obsession to harvest one of these majestic creatures.

The arrival of the deer hunting season is perhaps the most anticipated of all the hunting seasons I'd experienced during my years as a game warden. Deer hunters actively began preparing for the hunting season by sighting-in their rifles at the very first sign of a killer frost. That was followed by countless days of scouting and observing the habitat where the deer were plentiful—especially that big old "trophy buck" they hoped to bag before the season ended. I could easily tell when the deer season was approaching without ever looking at a calendar simply by observing the number of trucks on the highway with rifles hanging in a gun rack and the blaze orange hunting garb nearby. Prior to the legal hunting season, it was quite common to hear rifle shots ringing out from near and afar, as many serious hunters anxiously sighted-in their rifles, readying themselves for that opening day excitement. The local stores stocked up on ammo, snacks, hunting clothes and several books and magazines promoting the sport. The air of excitement was second to none. Employers were planning on a shortfall of workers from people calling in sick or taking their vacations in order to participate in the great Maine tradition.

Sadly, it appears that today's hunting is not like the great hunts of days gone by. It used to be quite common to travel about the countryside dodging the many vehicles parked along the road, abandoned by hunters who were out in the woods pursuing their prey. In the later years of my employment, it was getting harder and harder to find a hunter. It seems the family tradition of fathers, sons, and daughters joining together for a day's hunt no longer is as highly anticipated as it once was. Posted property, stricter rules and regulations, and the expense of taking time away from work to go hunting make it more and more difficult. Places where hunters were once allowed to roam freely in pursuit of their quarry had either been posted to all hunting activity, or turned into housing developments or other uses. Rules and regulations were constantly changing, as was the price of licenses to legally take part in the activity.

The deer herd still remains quite plentiful and abundant. However, the influx of the coyote roaming throughout the woods has certainly changed the habits of Maine's most sought-after big game animal.

There was no question the changing times seemingly have curtailed an old Maine tradition, one that many sportsmen used to live for. I was glad to have shared the experiences back in those days gone by when deer hunters were everywhere, and the air of excitement was high as we wardens ran from one complaint to another, trying to balance good public relations with the enforcement duties that often kept us hopping.

Wall-Mounted Trophies

A large rack, with glassy eyes staring off into space,
makes a good wall mount.

There is something a little macho about a deer hunter wanting to display on his living room wall, a mounted trophy deer head with a huge set of antlers. These well-designed mounts, fully equipped with a set of glass eyes staring off into space, occupied the walls of several Waldo County homes and a few area businesses. However, this phenomenon isn't limited to just Waldo County. It seems to be a tradition all across the country.

A perfect example of some of these mounts could be viewed at my favorite place for swapping hunting stories and a steady barrage of jokes—Thomas' Barber Shop, located in downtown Belfast. Folks flocked to this little barbershop, sitting back and listening to barbers George Campbell, Roy Thomas and Storm Gould telling tale after tale about the big bucks they've seen, shot, or that they've been attacked by. All the while, the walls of the crowded little shop were decorated by a large contingency of deer-head mounts staring down on them as they continued spewing their wild tales. Often, these stories got quite exaggerated and the conversations suddenly turned into one giant BS session among the customers seated in the chairs, all of them trying to outdo one another.

On more than one occasion, I found these stories to be far more entertaining than anything you could find on the television set. The trip to the local barber shop was always an anticipated adventure.

I especially recall a time when I was getting my hair trimmed. I was covered in the cloth garb used to keep the cut hair from covering a person from head to tail. George was giving me that haircut I so desperately needed. As he was snipping away, a couple of fellows were about to enter the shop.

George muttered, "Oh boy, here comes some fun, John! These two guys coming to the door claim to be the biggest poachers to ever set foot out on Islesboro." Islesboro was a small island located a few miles off the coast of Belfast, where the deer were plentiful, and the local law was typical of what an islander's interpretation happened to be at that moment. In other words, they were not the most law-abiding folks around! Those folks didn't always go right by the lawbook out on the 12 miles of rock.

George, assuming the men didn't recognize me as being the local game warden, deviously snickered and said, "We'll have some fun here!" George was always poking it to one of his regular customers in order to cause a little humorous conversation.

Exchanging the usual greetings as the men came through the door, George gave them a chance to hang up their coats and to get seated in among the rest of the clientele within the little shop. It wasn't long before George laid his little trap for the men he referred to as "the Island poachers."

"So, boys, how's the deer population out on the island? You ain't shot 'em all out there yet, have you?" he prodded his two customers, knowing that it was still a few weeks before the legal hunting season officially was to start.

"Not yet, but we've surely done all right," boasted Ernie, totally unaware that I was a warden.

George, never letting on whose hair he was cutting, boldly asked, "Aren't you fellas afraid the wardens will catch on to your activities and snap you up one of these nights while you're out there doing the dirty deed?"

"It'll never happen," Freddy chuckled, "I doubt they could ever sneak onto the island without us knowing it! We have a great system in place for knowing who is coming and who is going," he added.

About that time, George was finishing up with my haircut. He was about ready to give these fellows a little lesson on knowing who they were talking to before they began running their mouths. Before he could remove the cover from around my neck and lap, hiding the warden's uniform I was wearing, Ernie sputtered, "We got a nice buck the other night! It had a beautiful rack. One that would put these babies hanging on your wall to shame, George old boy!" he bragged.

It was show and tell time, as George vacuumed away the loose hairs from my shoulders and tore off the cover hiding my warden's uniform.

"Have you fellas ever met John Ford, our local game warden?" he smirked, as a sudden hush fell over the entire establishment.

Rather dumbfounded, and obviously in a mild state of shock, Freddy quickly said, "Nope, can't say that I have. It's nice to meet you, John!" Without so much as wasting a breath, he quipped, "George can vouch for the fact that we both are the biggest bull-shitters to ever come through the door of his shop, so don't believe all that you hear!"

It was a classic moment! Obviously a great comeback from the sudden predicament he found himself in. By now, the entire place was hysterically enjoying the moment. It was another of those classic moments that always seemed to prevail whenever I went to Thomas' Barber Shop, sharing some quality time with George, Roy, Storm, and the rest of the crew.

The mounted deer trophy head has become a symbol of manhood. A great sense of personal achievement for many a hunter. The hanging-head mount is conveniently displayed as a means of convincing others to recognize that the owner of the mount was a great hunting conqueror of sorts. The deer hunting ritual is a time when these hunting warriors can publicly show off their expert capabilities of how easily they can bag a trophy buck. The mounted deer-head is nothing more than positive proof of the great skill and expertise involved in the pursuit.

Family acceptance of one of these glassy-eyed wall decorations often comes with some rather stiff tension between the "Queen of the castle," and the "King himself."

The Queen opts for some fancy decoration from a home interior decorating party that she attended to place upon the wall. But the King firmly holds his ground, demanding the glassy-eyed monster be the only thing allowed in his den or hanging from the living room wall. Usually, the mount had to precisely be placed right over the chair where he'd spend most of his leisure time. After all, a trophy mount wasn't ever meant to be hidden by some pretty picture, or a wall plaque from a home decoration party—simply a symbol of something with no real story behind it.

Each wall mount comes with its share of tales, detailing just how the "great white hunter" outwitted the smartest of the old swamp bucks. In reality, probably the animal stupidly walked into the sights of a high-powered rifle and absolutely no hunting skill was involved. But then again, what hunter in his right mind would ever admit to pure luck when it comes to impressing his cronies as to his great hunting abilities? In most instances, bagging a trophy buck is nothing more than a mental battle between the hunter and the hunted! A battle whereby only the hunter and God himself knows what the real deal was. One thing for sure, in most cases the story gets inflated far more than what really happened. But the hunter has the proof staring down from the wall, strategically placed over his living room chair, and who's going to prove anything different?

You Guys Are NUTS!

By far, one of the most unusual deer hunting trophy situations I ever encountered involved a civil case that was brought to Belfast court by two local hunters. Both of them were vying for the top prize in a local big buck competition.

These contests are common throughout the state during the hunting season at many local mom-and-pop stores where hunters legally register their quarry. For a small entrance fee at the beginning of the season, hunters have the opportunity to win a nice prize for the biggest buck registered.

Prior to the strict gun registration requirements that we have today, one of the most common top prizes was a nice hunting rifle—always a sought after treasure for that hunter who thrives in his sport. The individual entrant who presented the largest buck for registration is the declared winner of the prize.

Most times, these contests conclude with no controversies or questions asked. Sometimes however, these competitions are downright crafty, enticing even the most honest of citizens into violating the rules in an effort to be known as the "top dog" of the group. It's a macho thing for that great white hunter who wants to impress his buddies as being the very best.

I recall one competition involving a major discrepancy over how much the testicles of a buck deer weighed. Seems as though these two local hunters had both entered the same big buck contest. Both of them were successful and weighed their deer on the same set of scales at the store running the contest. The overall weight of the two deer was extremely close, boiling down to a few ounces or less. One buck was weighed with the testicles intact, while the other was weighed with the prized jewels unattached. The deer with the testicles attached was declared the winner, causing a rather heated ruckus between the two parties involved. The matter was so contested, that it eventually ended up being heard before a judge at the Belfast District Court in a civil suit brought about by the losing party.

The entire issue boiled down to one specific detail: just how much does a buck's testicles weigh? It was a detail no one was able to scientifically verify. Even I was called in to testify, but I wouldn't touch the matter with a 10-foot pole. After all, what scientific claim did I have as being an expert on the weight of a deer's testicles?

The prize ended up being awarded to the hunter who had included the testicles in his quarry. The judge all but had the two men flip a coin to declare an official winner! But after hearing all of the evidence, he determined the weight of the deer's testicles wouldn't have made enough of a difference to reverse the decision made by the contest's sponsor. This hotly contested issue remains a serious bone of contention between these two hunters to this very day!

Personally, I felt they both were a little nuts—no pun intended. But then again, who was I to say!? I was only the local warden, not some expert with a degree in determining the weight of a buck's family jewels! That trial managed to bring a few snickers and smirks from those who jammed the crowded courtroom to witness this wildlife fiasco firsthand.

Who Really Are The Best Hunters in The Family?

The trophy buck – every family member wanted it!

During my tenure as a warden, Maine hunting laws allowed one deer per hunter to be killed per season. Each animal was required to be registered by the person who killed it at a designated tagging station within the jurisdiction of where the animal was taken. Upon completing and signing the official registration document making the kill legal, the registering person swears under oath that he or she is the person responsible for killing the animal being presented for registration. These deer registration stations were scattered over a wide area of my district. In most cases, it was the small mom-and-pop stores that welcomed the opportunity to tag deer, as the legal requirement brought a little extra business into their stores.

In some cases, town clerks were authorized to be the tagging agents at their homes. For example, the town clerk of Burnham,

Caroline Mitchell, was one of those who for years registered deer at her residence. Whenever I was at these agencies checking the tagging information, I wanted to see how many deer were being harvested and if the deer registered were being legally taken. There were always a few questionable issues as to the legal taking of these animals that would surface while I inspected the registration books.

For example, some deer presented to an agent for registration, according to the staff, were stiffer than a board, with rigor mortis already present in the animal. This was a sure sign that the animal was not a fresh kill as reported by the person registering it. According to the hunter, the deer was a fresh kill, but more than likely the animal had been killed long before ever being brought to the tagging station.

One of the amusing trends I noticed as I checked through the tagging books, was that at the start of the season the youngest of the children in a large family registered a deer first. Some of these young tykes were about as excited to be tagging their very first deer as they would be to go to the dentist to have a tooth pulled. Such a reaction was almost a dead giveaway that they were being dragged into the tagging station to register a deer they didn't shoot!

Occasionally there would be a young lady, a senior citizen, a disabled grandma or grandpa, or a distant relative who only minutes before arriving at the tagging station to tag a deer, had purchased a hunting license in order to legally register the kill. Sometimes these licenses were purchased less than 15 minutes before they arrived at the tagging station to register their prize. Even Superman couldn't buy his license, shoot and disembowel an animal, load it into a car, and tag it within 15 minutes of buying a license. It was truly amazing how quickly these nimrods were able to bag a critter, when most of the real serious hunters went for days on end without ever seeing anything.

Sometimes the deception involved the most honest and respectable citizens within our communities. One of my duties entailed checking these tagging books and looking for signs of obvious violations. I had to be extremely careful not to falsely accuse someone of wrongdoing without the facts to back up my accusations.

One hunting statistic that I found particularly interesting was how that first week of the four-week hunting season the women always seemed to out-shoot and out-hunt the men in the family. The registration books showed the females to be harvesting deer at a rate of 3-1 over their male counterparts. Certainly the registration books wouldn't reveal a possible falsehood, which left me to conclude that perhaps women were the more skilled hunters in our woods.

The second week of the hunting season, it seems the young kids in the family were the most successful hunters of the household. One by one, they registered their deer at the local tagging station. Many of them could hardly hold a rifle up to their shoulders, but obviously they had a better run of luck than poor old pop, who solemnly stood right alongside of them answering all of the questions required for the registration forms. A great way to teach youngsters the rules of honesty!

Finally, near the end of the season, Dad returned home with a whopping big buck of his own, thus ending a successful hunting season for the entire family. It was an annual tradition. The season provided a freezer filled with enough wild game meat to carry the entire family through the winter months. In some cases it provided Dad with yet another wall mount to hang over his head.

The deer season certainly provided this lawman with plenty of unusual and sometimes rather entertaining experiences. I anxiously anticipated its arrival almost as much as the hunters I'd be monitoring. The long and tedious fall months provided more than their fair share of memories. I certainly enjoyed every minute of being out there in the field, hearing and witnessing the stories and events firsthand.

With so many hunters in the woods, I dreaded having to respond to a hunting accident or to a search for some lost hunter. Thankfully, those types of incidents were not an everyday occurrence. In my 20 years of being on the beat, there was only one fatality that took up considerable investigation time. One was one more than enough!

For the most part, I thoroughly enjoyed the stories associated with a hunt! There were some real whoppers being told!

Them Damn Dam Builders

Throughout the state, a fair amount of a warden's time was spent removing nuisance beaver dams from flooded woodlots, or from some plugged highway culvert that was threatening the flow of traffic in a town.

There were times when I wondered why the good Lord placed these critters on Earth!

I often wondered for what practical purpose the good Lord ever placed these flat-tailed, furry, beady-eyed, aquatic creatures on Earth. There must have been a valid reason. But for the life of me I couldn't think of one. The beaver complaints seemed endless as I found myself wrestling with the sticks and mud while swatting large swarms of black flies and mosquitoes that thrived in such an environment. I rated these furry little dam-building engineers right up there with those damned old pesky mosquitoes and black flies. All of them are nothing more than miserable and irritable nuisances to those of us who were forced to deal with them.

Handling beaver issues constantly tried my patience and interfered with my daily routine of patrolling the woods and streams, searching for the so-called bad guys! Realistically though, I knew these oversized rodents actually were useful for our wildlife in many ways that I didn't want to admit. They were placed here for a reason, if for nothing more than to keep trying the patience of us wardens.

In some instances they provided a mild sort of living for trappers seeking their hides. There was a time when a prime beaver pelt paid $1 per square inch, rewarding an ambitious trapper extremely well for his hard-earned efforts. However, today those prices have dropped considerably, making the effort almost worthless.

A pesky beaver challenged my patience on more than one occasion. At times, I actually developed a pure hatred for the damn dam builders. Especially after I'd somehow created a major catastrophe using dynamite to blow up one of their cleverly crafted dams. For instance, I may have inadvertently blown up and washed out a bridge, and ripped apart a newly placed culvert, costing the taxpayers a small fortune to replace.

If only we could teach people to build a dam as easily as these creatures could, especially with the limited amount of materials and resources available to them. Just to watch them construct one of these structures in the short period of time it takes them is truly amazing.

Using materials consisting of nothing more than a few sticks, a little mud, and an occasional rock or two, overnight they've built a dam sturdy enough to flood an area, sufficiently meeting their needs. They had no bulldozers, no cranes, no shovels, or other mechanical items to assist them with the task. Their only means of transporting the various materials used in making such a fortress, was their paws, mouths, and sharp teeth.

An established beaver dam, located in a remote area of the woods, is beneficial to our wildlife. Some of the older beaver dams created along a brook or stream provide an excellent place for an angler to catch a nice mess of Brook trout, not to mention the various species of wildlife and waterfowl that seek out a beaver pond as a sanctuary for their own existence. Although I hate to admit it, a beaver dam that is established far away from civilization and one that is not interfering with the daily routine of mankind, actually is a great benefit to all of us. It's when they start interfering with man's activities that their efforts create a problem.

The patience and perseverance of these aquatic critters certainly are a hell of a lot better than mine. I found that with a few well-placed sticks of dynamite, I could flatten a beaver dam in a matter of seconds, only to return the next morning and find the damn thing built again. More often than not, the new structure was more solid and bigger than the one I'd removed the day before.

In an attempt to find a remedy to keep them from building back in the same spot, I was told by my friend and old time trapper Red Rines of Unity, "If you want to keep them beaver from building back in the same spot, John, just find yourself a dead porcupine," he sputtered. For the most part, Red was as knowledgeable in dealing with beaver and trapping them as anyone in the area. Surely his advice would be valid and worthy of consideration, I thought.

"What the hell would I do with a dead porcupine?" I rather bluntly inquired.

"If you find one, hang him upside down by his tail, off from a long stick placed in front of what's left of the beaver dam. Make sure you hang him nose down, so that his head is about 6 inches off from the water," he emphasized. "The stick supporting the dead quill pig needs to be placed at a 45-degree angle or less, secured roughly near the middle of the dam. I guarantee you, John boy, they'll never rebuild their dam in that spot! They'll depart the area forever.

"Now mind ya, this trick of the trade isn't completely fool proof, but you give it a try and then come back here and let me know what you think!" he smiled.

I trusted Red, and even though I couldn't for the life of me understand what the relationship between a beaver and a dead porcupine might be, I took him for his word.

For the next several days I searched the highways for a deceased "quill pig" flattened by a car. Any other time the highways were littered with them. But now, just because I wanted one, it was like looking for a pot of gold at the end of a rainbow. There just wasn't one to be found anywhere!

In the meantime, I constantly dug out and removed a beaver dam located in south Unity. They were continuously flooding a back road after plugging the culvert, night after night. I'd dig it out the first thing in the morning and they'd have it rebuilt by daybreak the next day. I even spent countless hours hiding with my shotgun, hoping to resolve the problem once and for all, but they never appeared while I was there.

Finally one day I found a dead porcupine on Route 9 in Troy. Quickly scooping up the smelly, dead critter I threw it in the back of my truck, heading for the beaver dam I'd been working on. Doing precisely as Red advised, I hacked down a nearby alder, firmly attaching the dead porcupine to the stake so that it was hanging nose down exactly as Red had stated. I drove the other end of the stake into the beaver dam, directly in front of the plugged culvert. I firmly secured the "quill pig" to the stake with leftover dynamite wire from one of my previous attempts of ridding the dam from the area. I couldn't wait to return the next morning to see if my old trapping buddy knew what the hell he was talking about.

The next day I returned to the area much earlier than normal, hoping the water wasn't flooding the road as it had so many times before. When I rounded the bend I couldn't believe my eyes. The road was flooded worse than ever. Those damn beavers had used the dead porcupine as a major building block for their efforts. The dead porky was buried deep in among a large pile of sticks and mud. I barely saw the end of his tail.

Momentarily, I envisioned my good friend Red with his head sticking into that pile of mud and sticks, and only the bottom of his boots showing. I bet he was sitting there at home with a big grin on his face, wondering if I'd fallen for his little "quill pig" theory. It looked like the old boy got me at a time when I was the most vulnerable—a moment when I was desperately seeking any possible remedy for this damn dam problem that was wasting my precious time. I should have learned long ago that sometimes when you are stressed and dealing with issues such as these, that even your best friends can make you look like an idiot. This was one of those times!

Those Rather Annoying Car/Deer Accidents

We wardens received calls at all hours of the day and night, requiring a response to cover a car/deer accident where some poor soul had collided with a deer while driving on one of our busy highways. In most cases, the incident was simply a case of property damage, where the vehicle was severely injured and the deer was deceased. All of these collisions required paperwork showing that the incident had been properly investigated—paperwork for the driver to present to his insurance company that legally established the collision was, in fact, with a deer or some other wild animal.

Occasionally some hoodlum who had tipped one too many beers at a party claimed to have hit a deer in order to have the insurance company make good on the claim for his wrecked car. More than once I investigated an accident where I knew there hadn't been a deer within 40 miles of the incident, but proving otherwise was difficult.

These vehicle-wild animal collisions always seemed to occur at the most inappropriate of times, usually right after I'd just crawled into bed seeking a good night's rest after working countless hours. When the bucks were in rut during the later part of the fall the accident rates increased. More than one of the testosterone-driven critters fell prey to the front end of a car or truck, never bothering to look where they were going as they actively pursued a nearby doe. Love was in the air and surely no mechanical monster was about to disrupt that loving courtship these creatures were seeking!

When I got one of these calls, most of the time my poor wife, Judy, would patiently listen to my bitching and bellowing in the middle of the night as I floundered around in the darkness, trying to get suited up to respond to the complaint. Many times she simply turned a deaf ear, ignoring my grumblings and profanity-laced complaints, while I banged around the house in a comatose state, gathering up my gear. There were times, however, when her patience wasn't quite as forgiving as I had hoped it would be. It was those moments of family tension that caused me to hit the highway like a whipped pup without a bone, and all of it caused because I'd ranted a little louder and longer than what she cared to hear. The sharp tongue lashings I received from the queen of the house were well deserved, especially after I'd made everyone else in the household just as miserable as I was at two or three o'clock in the morning. Even the dog was giving me dirty looks!

I wouldn't dare say how many of these collisions I covered over my career, but I would confirm that on just about every one of them I complained about having to respond. I fully suspect that I wasn't the only warden in the state who had that type of a negative attitude!

Don't Take Your Kid With You

Undoubtedly the proudest moment of my life was the birth of my son, John Jr. I highly anticipated those days when I could take him out on patrol with me, so that he could see what a great career I had chosen.

One afternoon when Little John was about 4 years old, I received a report of a car/deer accident in the town of Winterport. Winterport was not my patrol area, but the district warden who normally covered the area was on a day off, so I was the closest official to handle the complaint. I could tell by the way Little John was acting that he wanted to go with me if I'd let him. The fact that he was standing by the kitchen door with his coat in his hands and his hat on were pretty good indicators! I recognized the call as being a good chance to give his mother a little break in her child-rearing routine and likewise, I'd hopefully have a little private time with junior. After all, I was only going to nearby Winterport, where I'd be making out the necessary paperwork and then coming right back home. What harm could it do to take my son along with me? It would be a little enjoyable time for a father and son get together.

Arriving at the scene of the collision, we were greeted by a very distraught lady who claimed she had accidentally struck a small fawn as it crossed the road in front of her. The damages to her vehicle were minimal.

Hysterically, she cried, "The poor little thing has crawled out of the road and is down there in the alders somewhere. He's dragging his hind quarters, and I don't think he will live," she wailed.

With Little John trotting along behind me, we headed down over the bank and into the alders, searching for the poor injured critter along the way. Quietly sneaking through the thick alders,

I saw the cute little fawn lying ahead of us. It was quite obvious he was unable to use his hind quarters and that I'd have to dispatch him, putting him out of his misery. The fawn was blatting and flailing around, desperately trying to drag himself away from our impending approach. Eventually, he ended up half in and half out of a nearby stream. Pathetically he stared at us with those large brown eyes, as we slowly inched his way. I knew what had to be done.

Placing Little John out of harm's way, I slowly removed my handgun, instructing John to cover his ears. I explained to JJ as best I could why it was necessary to dispatch the fawn so that it wouldn't suffer anymore. I quickly fired three shots from my service revolver, causing the wounded deer to take its last breaths of fresh air.

Little John however, found plenty of fresh air, as he began screeching at the top of his lungs, calling me a murderer, a killer, and several other angrily mumbled insults he had tucked away in that young mind of his. He made it perfectly clear that he didn't love me anymore, as he continued screeching at the top of his lungs! By now I feared the bystanders who had gathered out along the highway would think I'd just shot my own kid, as I desperately tried getting him to calm down. No amount of discussion was about to persuade Little John that I'd done the right thing! I tried telling him how it was so much better to end the suffering for the poor little fawn, rather than to have him die a slow and painful death. But my words were falling upon deaf ears. He obviously had inherited the trait from his mother, as I'd seen her do the same thing on a few occasions when I was trying to explain something sensible to her.

John yowled and screeched all the way back to my cruiser, as I dragged the little fawn behind us. My heart was aching like never before, as I watched those tears of sorrow sliding down my son's cheeks. A son who by now was viewing his father as being the most evil man on earth.

I silently thought to myself, "Why? Why in hell did I bring him along with me to see something like this? Why couldn't it have been a normal car/deer accident, with the dead animal laying alongside of the road?"

As if my son's screeching and fit of anger weren't bad enough, the lady who struck the deer was even worse—not so much for my killing the deer, which she knew had to be done, but for having my young son being forced to witness the incident. She was making idle threats about filing a complaint with the department as to my serious lack of parenting skills. Maybe she was completely justified, because I was beginning to doubt them myself.

Once inside the cruiser, John never spoke to me during the entire trip back home, no matter how hard I tried to smooth things over. He just sat there, pouting, sniffling, and sobbing to himself, staring straight out through the passenger side window of my cruiser. So much for having good intentions and trying to impress upon my son as to what a great job I had!

The next day he somewhat softened his hard stance by giving me a half-hearted hug before I headed off to work. I think his mother had been privately counseling him on the facts of life when I wasn't around. I didn't know whose heart was aching the most—his or mine.

Look - Damn It, I Just Came By There!

Another one of those vehicle-deer complaints occurred one Halloween night after I had worked straight ahead for 30 hours or more without a break. I'd finally managed to crawl in between the sheets for some much-needed rest. It was roughly 2:45 in the morning when I finally arrived home. My head had no more than hit the fluffy pillow before I was out like a light. I couldn't recall a time when I'd been more exhausted.

That much-needed rest didn't last long however, as I was jolted awake by a loud ringing right next to my ear. Answering the contraption in a groggy and very disgusted voice, I muttered a weak, "Hello!"

The rather chipper voice on the other end of the line inquired, "Hi! Is this the game warden?"

I felt like saying, "No it isn't. You've got the wrong number!" and hanging up, but I knew better. I sputtered a sleepy, "Yes it is!"

"Well, hello there, warden, this is so and so from Unity College, and I have a slight problem!" he happily chirped, acting as if the whole world should have been up at that insane hour of the day.

By then, I was getting a might bit irritated as to just how jovial this pre-dawn idiot appeared to be. Didn't he know I'd just gone to bed and that it was 3:30 in the morning? He was about to have a problem all right, and it was going to be a hell of a lot worse than anything he was calling me for.

I bluntly inquired, "What do you want?"

In that same jovial tone as before, he replied, "Well sir, it seems as though I just struck a big buck at the foot of Quaker Hill up here in Unity. I got a little damage on the old buggy, but the deer is still alive, laying here in the ditch! I don't suppose I could call upon you to come over here and dispatch it for me, could I?" he deviously snickered.

Still in a half-comatose state of mind, I screeched as loudly as I could, "Look gawdamn it, I just came down through there a few minutes ago! Why to hell didn't you hit it while I was there?"

There was nothing but a dead silence on the other end of the phone line.

By then I was starting to wake up a bit more, realizing that his situation was real and whether I wanted to or not, I really needed to go out.

Disgustedly I barked, "Damn it, don't you go anywhere, I'll be right out," and with that I slammed the phone down.

As I got dressed, I suddenly realized how rude and unprofessional I'd been to this poor guy. I knew I owed him a sincere apology once I arrived at his location. I just hoped he was understanding enough to accept my lame excuse for being as rude as I'd been. After all, how was he supposed to know that I'd been awake for more than 30 hours?

As I pulled into the area, I observed a vehicle parked along the side of the road, with its emergency flashers going. I noticed the driver was slumped low behind the steering wheel, cautiously watching my every move through his rear view mirror as I approached. He barely cracked his window so I could verbally communicate with him, while at the same time, he was eye-balling my every move with sheer skepticism. I could tell that he was about as nervous as a young buck about ready to go under the knife for a vasectomy. I couldn't blame him!

I quickly apologized for my rude rant over the telephone, as I desperately tried explaining my serious lack of sleep. I was speaking through a small opening in the window, as I pleaded my case for being only half awake when he called. I hoped to break the ice, reassuring him that I wasn't the mad man he'd spoken to only minutes before. Finally, through the power of gentle persuasion, I was able to coax my friend to reluctantly step outside of his vehicle.

He pointed to the ditch where the injured deer lay, barely breathing. I quickly removed my service revolver, dispatching the big buck to put it out of its misery. Within minutes, I'd completed all of the paperwork, helped my new friend load the nice 10-point buck into his trunk and sent him along his way. He appeared to be happier than a pig in slop. I only wish I felt the same way.

But in the end, all is well that ends well! Responding to his needs actually worked out far better than I anticipated. On the way back home, I happened upon a night hunter sneaking out of a back field. He was in the act of illuminating the field as I rounded the bend. The fact he had desperately attempted to flee the area with a loaded rifle snuggled up beside him, was enough to determine his intent. It looked as if that comfortable bed back home would be empty for a while longer.

The Doughnut Wagon and the Buck

Perhaps one of the more unusual deer/vehicle collisions we covered was when Warden Gilbert and I were working together near the town of Newport.

It too was real early in the wee morning hours, well before sunrise. The state police dispatcher advised us that a gentleman operating a bread delivery truck had struck and killed a deer on the interstate while on his route to Bangor to make a delivery of bread products. The complainant had possession of the deer and requested to meet with us as soon as possible to fill out the necessary paperwork.

We met at Shorette's Diner, a small luncheon establishment just off the interstate in Newport. The diner was open 24 hours a day, catering to the many truckers traveling along the interstate and to folks like us who occasionally had to put on the feed bag in the middle of the night. We pulled into the diner and met the complainant inside the restaurant. Over a light breakfast and a quick cup of coffee, we filled out the necessary paperwork entitling him to possess the deer. Rather excitedly, he told us the large buck was stuffed in the back of his delivery truck, in among the doughnuts and fresh bread that he was supposed to deliver in Bangor. He planned to make his deliveries as quickly as possible and return home, where he would take care of the carcass.

Finishing our light breakfast, we exited the restaurant together. In the parking lot, Norman stated, "I probably ought to take a look at your deer, just so that I can honestly say we have investigated this incident."

There was little or no damage to the delivery truck as far as he could tell. As we approached the wagon, there was a hellish thrashing commotion coming from within the windowless truck. Swinging the back doors open, a huge buck deer sailed out through the opening at full speed, sailing right in between us. The large antlered beast nearly bowled us over as he shot out across the parking lot at a speed equivalent to that of a race horse running in the Kentucky Derby.

Apparently, as we sat inside the restaurant having our light lunch, the unconscious deer came around and had been thrashing all about the caged prison he found himself in. Inside the truck were several ripped loaves of bread and crushed doughnuts spread all over the floor. The damaged products appeared to be covered with small brown droppings. Droppings that I wouldn't exactly classify as raisins!

Needless to say, the poor truck driver was quite distraught as to this sudden turn of events.

"How to hell am I ever going to explain this to the boss?" he quietly mumbled to himself. There was no doubt about it, he had a serious problem on his hands.

As for the deer, it continued across the parking lot and back toward the interstate highway from whence it came, only a few miles to the north from where it was originally picked up!

Several months later, I happened upon that same driver. Only that time he was driving a large brown truck that said UPS on its side. I didn't dare ask, but always wondered if this career change may have been the result of some damaged goods in his last line of employment.

Over the years I've certainly covered my fair share of car/deer accidents, probably no more than any other warden in the state, though, as we all had more than our fair share of damaged vehicles and dead critters to take care of.

Just for the record, I actually was involved in a collision or two of my own with the very species I spent most of my time protecting. None of us were exempt!

During my long career there was an opportunity to investigate a few rather unusual vehicle/deer collisions—for example, there was a snowmobile/deer collision that occurred on a remote trail in the town of Thorndike. It involved a young man who earlier that day had been in District Court paying a hefty fine for riding his snow machine on the highways. Maybe he was safer by breaking the law and cruising the highways instead of chancing a collision on the narrow snowmobile trails! Fortunately he was not injured. But the deer was dead and the snowmobile was in dire need of some major repairs.

Then there was an occasional deer/train collision that required removal of a smashed carcass from the tracks.

There was a motorcycle/deer collision, which fortunately for the operator resulted in only a few minor bruises and abrasions. The motorcycle, however, didn't fare quite so well!

But probably the most interesting incident I recall was a plane/deer collision that occurred at the airport in Pittsfield. Other than a great deal of damage to the small plane, and a change of underwear for the occupants, no people were injured.

Yup, there's no question about it, those damn deer collisions with man's mobile toys were at times some of the biggest pains in the butt that we wardens had to contend with.

The timing required to investigate them never seemed to be right. Not that I ever expected it would be!

The Big Blowout

On March 11, 1981, I departed the house believing it would be another boring and quiet day on patrol. I headed for Augusta for some minor repair work to be done to my cruiser. It was a quiet time of the year for us game wardens. The winter snow was quickly melting and the onslaught of spring was right around the corner. Before long most of us would be busy again, quietly perched along some small freshwater brook working fishermen pursuing a mess of smelts, night after night.

The annual run of freshwater smelts was a springtime attraction for sportsmen in the area. It was an opportunity for men who had been cooped up at home all winter to eagerly anticipate the chance to go outside and let their hair down with friends along some remote smelt brook. Many of them could not care less about catching a mess of smelts. Instead they were anxious to roam freely outside in the middle of the night, and to party with old comrades after a long and cold winter. It was that anticipation of a "boys' night out" that brought most of them to the local smelt brook every spring. The smelts were a little something extra, a little something to take home to mother, proving to her where they'd been for the evening.

On this day, as I was cruising toward Augusta I was engrossed in thought, reminiscing about my great lifestyle and how much I was enjoying my career. I was fulfilling that youthful dream of being a Maine game warden, and after 11 years was still doing it with that same burning desire I had from day one. I certainly had been blessed in my daily life.

The police radio was blaring away with its usual chatter of various law enforcement agencies from around the state. There was a constant flow of communication with the troopers and wardens who were being dispatched to accident scenes and other incidents that needed attention from my brothers in uniform.

As I headed for Augusta, I vaguely overheard a radio broadcast advising all units to be on the lookout for two escaped inmates who had walked away from the Warren State Prison. The state police dispatcher stated these two criminals were considered the prime suspects in the theft of a pickup truck the previous night from a location near the prison compound. There was a possibility they might be armed and dangerous, the police broadcast advised.

During the 11 years I'd been on the job, there was one thing I learned rather quickly. The peace and tranquility of any given moment could, and would, change in the blink of an eye. In the world of law enforcement, boredom often was quickly replaced with a sheer adrenaline rush and plenty of hair-raising excitement.

But surely on this morning, as I slowly hiked my way toward Augusta, nothing would mess with the monotonous day that I'd already planned. After all, I was away from my patrol area, seeking to have a little maintenance done on the cruiser. I met up with a good buddy from warden school days, Warden Lloyd Perkins, at the local garage where we brought our cruisers in for repairs. Lloyd was just leaving the facility after having some work done on his cruiser.

"Jump in," he said, "I'll bring you back later when your cruiser's ready to go!"

Sounded good to me. It beat the hell out of standing around the garage. Together we headed to the Federal Street storehouse to see if there was any new equipment we might be able to scrounge away from the department's tightly run bargain bin.

The storehouse was the place we all seemed to congregate whenever we were in town. Trying to get any new equipment away from there was like hoping to win the lottery without ever buying a ticket. Those in charge of issuing the equipment and supplies were about as tight as the bark on an old oak tree. It had to be that way, otherwise those of us who were self-admitted pack rats would empty the establishment within a matter of hours.

While we were standing around the storehouse chatting, Lloyd received a message from the Maine State Police requesting assistance. The stolen truck from the Warren area had just been spotted at the shopping plaza west of the city. The dispatcher believed the two escaped inmates were inside the Sears store on a shopping spree. We were the closest units to that location, if we were available. So much for a quiet, boring day!

Rather than having a confrontation with these men inside the store and placing the public in harm's way, we sped up to the parking lot, waiting for them to return back to the stolen truck. Hopefully, by that time more units would arrive, thus preventing their escape.

As we pulled into the huge parking lot, the vehicle with the two escapees on board was just leaving the area. There was no question they'd spotted our uniforms, as they quickly accelerated, shooting out through the exit as if they were in the Daytona 500. Lloyd quickly pulled in behind them, signaling for them to stop. The chase was on! We sailed out of the parking lot in hot pursuit at speeds that were mind-boggling and damn right scary.

In the past, I'd been in on a few chases. For most of them, I was the one behind the wheel and had complete control over my own destiny. But on this day, I was simply along for the ride. My future depended upon Lloyd's driving skills behind the wheel. My butt was sucked to the passenger-side seat of his vehicle like a big mosquito hooked to a ripe and bloody vein. I have to be honest, it's a different situation when you're cruising along at warp speeds as a helpless passenger. You place your complete trust and faith in your partner, hoping to hell he can do as well as what you'd be doing if you were the one in control.

We found ourselves flying along back roads, heading away from Augusta toward the city of Gardiner. We were darting in and out of traffic, pursuing the two suspects who so desperately were trying to get away from us. The screaming siren and high speeds alerted many folks who were standing along the roadside, as we blew by them in a blur. Not being too familiar with the area, I didn't have a clue where we were—where we were going, or what to expect next. The passenger in the fleeing vehicle was maintaining a constant wary-eye out through the back window, obviously hoping to put a lot more distance between us. Likewise, I kept a stern eye toward him, hoping they weren't armed and that bullets wouldn't soon be flying our way.

Meanwhile, several state and local police units were coming our way from everywhere, hoping to bring this situation to a successful closure. Lloyd was maneuvering the cruiser like a redneck driver at that NASCAR race I spoke of earlier, as we continued over the narrow country roads at high speeds. Thank God it was Lloyd's district and he knew where we were going. If anything, we were gaining on these fugitives as they desperately attempted to make a clean get-away.

Eventually, we ended up at the busy intersection of the Gardiner/Randolph Bridge. The chase came to a sudden and rather abrupt halt, squarely in the middle of the road. With cars full of innocent and startled citizens frozen in place all around us, we skidded broadside to avoid colliding with the truck. Several police officers were arriving from the opposite direction, just as these subjects jumped out of the truck in an effort to make a mad dash to freedom.

I quickly tackled the escaped passenger on my side the moment his big clod-hoppers hit the paved highway. Lloyd had done the same thing to the fleeing felon on the other side of the street. A brief scuffle ensued between us as we toppled to the ground in a heap, with other police officers quickly rallying to our aid.

It had to have been quite a show for those unsuspecting citizens who happened to have been halted by the exciting scenario suddenly unfolding around them. There's nothing like a little drama to go with your Egg McMuffin and coffee in the morning, seeing that the local McDonald's restaurant filled with breakfast customers was within sight of this fiasco!

During this brief scuffle, I felt a major rush of cool air blowing onto my posterior. It was a rather cold feeling that really felt out of the norm! My department-issued wool pants no longer could completely encase that bulky frame I now found myself sporting after the long winter months. That skinny, 165-pound body I'd managed to carry for so many years had succumbed to an abrupt physical change. Prior to now, I was in denial that my pants were too small for that new weight gain I'd amassed. In other words, I'd just experienced a major blowout. And I'd done it right in front of God and the public who had witnessed this fiasco. I never wanted to let go of that youthful, slim and trim figure I possessed 11 years earlier.

As I was struggling with the detainee in the middle of the road, those folks who were stuck in traffic by the blocked road were getting a good look at my now exposed buttocks as we flip-flopped around on the ground. Not since the day when my State trooper buddy, Dennis Hayden, ripped his uniform britches during a scuffle with a couple of armed robbers in Benton, had such an embarrassing event occurred. At that time, I remember hysterically laughing at him as he desperately tried to maintain some form of personal dignity, with the arse end of his pants exposed for the entire world to see. He didn't seem to see the sense of humor back then, and I now knew exactly how he felt. That old adage of "what goes around, comes around" is true, I guess. The big difference being that Dennis' situation happened in front of a few of us cops and the two armed robbers who were in custody, and not the entire community. I felt as though the entire population of Gardiner and Randolph was witnessing this sorry side show.

Needless to say, within a few brief minutes the two escapees were on their way back to the crowbar hotel where they belonged. Just as quickly, Lloyd and I were headed back to the Federal Street storehouse, where I could hopefully plead my case for, at the very least, a new set of britches. Perhaps, maybe even a new and complete wardrobe!

So much for a routine day of boredom—this particular morning proved to be yet another memorable moment for the diaries. This incident wasn't the last time I chased escapees from the Maine State Prison. Within a few short months, "The Great Moody Mountain Manhunt" occurred in the rural community of Searsmont. Those escapees were on foot. They were far more dangerous and they were armed. One of them had nothing to lose, as he was serving a life sentence for the brutal and sadistic murder of a young boy a few years before.

It was during that nerve-racking time when I honestly felt that my career was about to come to a rather abrupt and tragic end. State trooper Dennis McLellan, with his faithful K-9, Ben, and I found ourselves staring down the barrel of their rifle, as escapees held us at gunpoint while we were chasing them through the woods. These fleeing escapees wounded Ben, but miraculously Dennis and I escaped unharmed.

Five days later, during a torrential downpour, State trooper Dennis Hayden, accompanied by his K-9, Skipper, and I were able to corral these men in the same way they had ambushed us earlier. We were onto them like a tick on a moose before they knew we were even around.

That time, they got to see what it was like to stare down the barrel of a loaded firearm!

Being a game warden turned out to be everything I thought it would be back when I was on the outside looking in. It was that anticipation of the unknown, the hype of excitement from one minute to the next, that I found to be the most appealing aspect of the great career I'd chosen. Thank God I kept the diaries to remember those moments when things quickly went from sheer boredom to a complete adrenaline rush.

I definitely was living the dream! Who could possibly ask for anything more?

Perhaps a Little Revenge

Trying to find illegal activity in May within my patrol area was sometimes a fruitless task. Other than a few fishermen seeking a mess of trout from a remote stream, most of the time it was extremely boring. In the spring of 1981, I was concentrating my efforts at the end of the Webster Cemetery Road in Troy. There was a fair amount of fishing activity along a small remote trout stream there. The area contained a decent supply of easy-to-catch and extremely small native brook trout.

On May 30, 1981, I noticed a pickup truck parked near the stream. I assumed the vehicle belonged to fishermen somewhere along the stream. I stationed myself nearby, patiently waiting for the owner of the truck to return to his vehicle. If nothing else, I'd at least impress upon these folks that their local game warden was keeping a watchful eye on the resources.

Eventually I heard voices coming my way. I observed two men carrying fishing poles and a small knapsack. As they trotted along the narrow footpath, I stepped out from the bushes to check their licenses. From the shocked looks on their faces, it was obvious something fishy, no pun intended, was going on. Then, in one swift motion, they tossed their knapsack into the tall ferns along the edge of the foot trail, obviously hoping I hadn't seen the overt action.

Their licenses were in order and I slowly sauntered over to where the knapsack was concealed in the tall ferns. I was very familiar with both of these men and never would have expected them to cross the line from legal to illegal. As a matter of fact, they both were what I considered to be as good friends. However, upon retrieving the knapsack, I found 22 brook trout, six more than the legal possession allowed by law. Also included in the catch were 11 short trout that were well below the legal six-inch limit as required by the fishing rules. The 11 short fish were two to four inches in length, hardly enough to satisfy a small fish hawk, let alone a couple of grown men. There wasn't enough meat on these little minnows to pry out of their teeth with the smallest toothpick in the world. It made absolutely no sense to be keeping fish this tiny, other than to see how many of the tiny trout they could catch. In doing so, they were robbing the small stream of its future stock of brook trout for others to enjoy in the years ahead.

I quickly wrote a couple of citations, holding these men responsible for their sins. They were quite humbled and embarrassed for the predicament they suddenly found themselves in. They made no excuses for their actions.

The friendship was never adversely affected because of this incident. They are as good friends today as they were before, although we've never discussed that particular incident between us whenever we get together. Had it been a personal issue for them, I'd have simply assumed that they were not the great friends I thought they were for having placed me into such a predicament in the first place. I had a job to do and an oath that I'd taken, swearing to treat everybody fairly. This was one of those awkward times when I was forced to stick to my guns.

On June 2, 1981, I returned to the same area. This time I located a nearby resident fishing in the brook without a license. He too was harvesting more than a few of these small brookies for reasons he couldn't explain. As I made out the citations to court, the conversation turned into a fairly heated discussion. He made a couple of idle threats, assuring me that in the days ahead I'd come to regret what I was doing.

"Would you care to explain what you mean by that? And what makes you think you have the right to fish here without a license, when everybody else is required to have one?" I calmly inquired.

He refused to respond to my inquiries, as he quickly snapped the citation out of my hands, storming back to his vehicle in a huff, mumbling and cursing along the way. It seemed like a strange encounter for someone who obviously knew he was in the wrong, but I'd let the courts decide the issue should he request a trial.

On June 4, 1981, I planned to check a remote beaver pond a few miles away from this little stream. Rumor had it that a few fishermen had located this remote beaver pond and were capturing several brookies from its waters. The beaver flowage was in an area that few people knew anything about, including myself.

Per protocol, I notified the state police via the radio, that I'd be out of my vehicle in Troy, and unavailable for calls. I actually had planned a double mission for that particular morning. The previous day I'd promised Trooper Reitchel, who lived in Troy, to tend to his dog while he was away visiting family. I planned to swing by his residence after checking this beaver flowage.

Upon locating the old beaver pond, there was no doubt it was being fished heavily, as evidenced by the amount of broken fishing line and empty bait containers left along the water's edge.

I thoroughly enjoyed poking around a beaver flowage. It's a natural place to view the several species of game that often congregate around the water's edge. The sacred place was kind of like a wildlife sanctuary that Mother Nature had provided for her clientele. There were a pair of ducks paddling along the water at the far end of the pond, cautiously watching my every move. A half-dozen turtles quickly slid off a couple of decaying water-soaked logs and frogs hopped around my feet in an attempt to scurry out of the way when I hiked on past them. As often happens in a place like this, a damned old snake slithered out from underneath my feet, sending a chill up my spine. They always gave me the heebie-jeebies, especially if I didn't see them well in advance. I think I'd actually like and admire the damn things if they'd only stand up and walk like any normal creature, instead of awkwardly slithering across the ground as they do.

There were a few deer and even a moose track along the muddy banks. It was as peaceful a place as imaginable, one where I felt as though I was the only human around. After an hour or so of floundering around this new-found haven, I eventually returned to my cruiser ready to re-enter the real world once again.

Upon starting the vehicle, I heard a steady stream of highly-excited police radio traffic. The state police dispatchers were busily relaying messages from a squad of officers and emergency personnel that appeared to be heading to the scene of some incident happening nearby. I overheard several wardens, state troopers, and the Unity Ambulance crew chatting back and forth seeking directions on where to go. I even heard Trooper Reitchel, whom I assumed to already being out of state, advising the responding officers as to where he thought a certain road in Troy was located. They appeared to be headed for the same Cemetery road in Troy that I'd been so intently covering the previous few weeks.

I felt a rush of excitement knowing that I wasn't far away, as I patiently waited for a moment to chirp in on the radio and offer my assistance. Finally, there was a lull in the radio traffic, allowing me to inquire what was going on.

State Trooper Greg Myers anxiously responded, "Where are you? Are you OK?"

I advised him of my location, while thinking to myself, "Why wouldn't I be OK? Hell, I've just been hiking around in God's kingdom for the past hour without a worry in the world."

"I never thought I'd be so damn glad to hear your voice," he responded. "We are responding to a report of a warden supposedly being shot near that area. Naturally, we assumed it was you."

It seems some deranged person had placed a bogus call to either the Maine State Police or to the Waldo County Sheriff's

Department, claiming a game warden had been shot near the cemetery in Troy. Seeing as where this was my patrol area, ironically it turned out that through all of this hyped up excitement, I was the object of the search. The only "threats" I'd experienced that warm spring morning were from a few curious ducks, a couple of painted turtles, several frogs, and that damned old slithering snake. And they were no real threat!

This search in progress was obviously a hoax, a sick joke played by someone who more than likely got a cheap thrill from watching nearby the reaction they'd created. I recalled that idle threat from the local fisherman a couple of days earlier. Perhaps this was that subtle form of revenge that he so blatantly spoke about, when he voiced his off-the-wall comment and displeasure for receiving a citation. Moreso, maybe it was a threat to keep law enforcement away from the stream where he found himself becoming a victim of the times.

I later heard that my prime suspect was a devoted scanner buff, constantly monitoring the police and fire frequencies, listening to the happenings going on in the area. There was little doubt in my mind who instigated the bogus call, but the burden of proof was such that in all likelihood he would skate by. And skate by he did!

Whoever had instigated the false report appeared to be sending a message that the little stream in Troy was off limits to any game warden wearing a badge and intent on protecting the resources for others to enjoy. This sick-minded prank lit my fire all the more as I vowed to camp in that area for the next few weeks. I certainly hoped a warden's life wasn't worth sacrificing over a few short trout or for a fishing without a license case. But in this day and age, one never knew anymore! The times were certainly changing and these changes were not for the best.

A few years before this incident occurred, two Idaho game wardens, Conley Elms and William Pogue, were brutally murdered by an illegal trapper they were attempting to arrest.

They were ambushed and shot in the head, execution style, by the trapper they had confronted. One of the warden's bodies was thrown into a nearby river, while the other was hidden in a coyote den. The perpetrator, Claude Dallas, was eventually arrested and tried for the murders of these fine officers, only to be regarded as a folk hero in the area where he came from.

Tragic incidents such as this, were a stark reminder of how quickly our country was changing its ways and, moreso, its thinking. In my opinion it wasn't for the better! Even right here in Maine, in 1922, two of our own Maine game wardens were murdered by a Canadian beaver trapper. Their bodies weren't found until the following spring when the ice melted out of the beaver pond where the murderer had dumped their remains. The suspect in that murder was never captured and held responsible for his actions, as he fled back across the border into Canada.

Violence on members of my own agency was nothing new. In 1886, two wardens were executed by a couple of men who were illegally using dogs to hunt deer. Another warden was shot and killed point blank by night hunters, as he was in the process of apprehending them in the wee morning hours. So nothing is surprising today when it comes to law enforcement issues and some of the clientele we wardens are forced to deal with.

This sick prank became yet another memory for the diaries. Sadly it was one without any sort of humor. But at least the day ended with a happy conclusion—for that I could be thankful.

Actually in the long run, I ended up paying dearly for the welcomed police support, as I was shamed into footing the bill for my buddies in blue uniforms as we all gathered for lunch at a local diner in Unity.

Once again, life was good and I found myself enjoying every bit of it. By the way, did I happen to mention just how much those boys in blue can eat, especially when it's a free lunch? Pay I did! They had me secured in a soft mood, and as such, they seized the moment. But in a subtle way it was a small price to pay, knowing that once again those of us wearing a law enforcement uniform really did care about one another. We rallied in support of each other during those times of crisis. This had been one of those times!

Thank God, it was a dress rehearsal and not the real McCoy!

She Was a Real Beauty

Looking back in the diaries, 1976 was off to a great start. It seemed as though my warden's career was moving forward much faster than I ever realized. The exciting adventures in the law enforcement profession managed to create new memories almost on a daily basis.

One snowy February night in 1976 brought yet another classic memory for the diaries.

Maine State Police Cpl. Dave Lindahl was visiting at our residence for a little chit-chat and a hot cup of coffee. It was snowing heavily outside when Dave arrived at the front door. Dave was a close and personal friend. We both started our careers at about the same time.

The outside activity was nil, the corporal stated, as we sat around the kitchen table chatting and enjoying a laugh or two, when suddenly the telephone rang.

The State Police dispatcher in Augusta directed Dave to head for the Winterport area as soon as possible. Trooper Bruce Dow was in pursuit of a drunk driver who was refusing to stop.

"Grab your coat and let's go!" Dave stated. He didn't have to ask twice. I enjoyed being in on the wild action—and it sounded as though this situation had the potential of being just that.

It was nearly blizzard conditions outside as we quickly scraped the ice from the cruiser windows and exited the driveway, headed for Winterport. The roads were treacherous enough in these snowy conditions for a sober driver and I couldn't imagine a drunk driver trying to navigate through the blowing snow on such a wild night.

On the way to assist Bruce, we monitored the radio communications between Trooper Dow and the barracks. It sounded as though they were not traveling very fast, but the female operator simply was refusing to stop.

Dave skillfully maneuvered the cruiser through the foothills of Monroe as we headed toward Winterport. I struggled trying to keep my butt firmly stuck to the seat. I figured any moment we could pitch out into the pucker-brush, as the cruiser skidded along the narrow snow-covered country road.

The flashing blue lights cast an eerie glow as they reflected off the falling snowflakes. Fortunately there was little traffic on the road. Normal folks were comfortably snuggled inside their homes during this major white-out.

Bruce apparently was directly behind the offending motorist, with the cruiser's lights flashing and the siren blaring as they traveled up one country road and down another.

"There are two people in the vehicle, a female operator, and a male passenger. The male passenger appears to be passed out," Bruce calmly informed the dispatchers. It was impossible for him to obtain the car's registration due to the snowy conditions.

Dave made excellent time, as we shot through Monroe village moving on toward Winterport. We were getting closer to the action with each passing second. At an intersection off the Goshen Road in Winterport, Trooper Dow stated, "They've gone into the ditch and can't get out. I'll be out of the car, Augusta!"

The radio was dead silent for what seemed like eternity as we imagined just what might be happening. I felt the adrenaline pumping into my veins and the excitement rising, as we continued sliding across the slippery, snow-covered roads, waiting to hear whether Bruce was all set. We were a few miles away from his location when suddenly an excited Trooper Dow was back on the radio, requesting assistance as soon as possible.

"The female operator is definitely intoxicated, Augusta," he shouted. "She's locked all of the doors in the vehicle and she won't let me in. Her male friend is passed out alongside of her, and she's got a shotgun stuffed in between the seats," he anxiously reported.

That old pucker factor suddenly increased, as the thoughts of dealing with a drunk female armed with a shotgun passed through my mind. Dave notified the barracks we'd be on scene shortly.

Off in the distance, we observed the flashing blue lights from Trooper Dow's cruiser penetrating the snowy skyline. We shot up the narrow road heading for his location. We were slipping and sliding every which way, as Dave desperately attempted to maintain a straight line of travel. Looming ahead of us in the roadway was Trooper Dow's vehicle. The offending car was parked at a precarious angle in the ditch right alongside the police cruiser.

As we pulled in behind them, Trooper Dow yelled, "She's locked the doors and refuses to talk. She claims the shotgun is loaded and that she isn't afraid to use it," he anxiously added.

We approached the car with extreme caution, while directing the beams of our flashlights inside the vehicle. The male passenger was definitely passed out, as he lay motionless on his side of the car. Either that or he was dead! The female driver, on the other hand, was screaming a tirade of foul-mouthed obscenities as she peeked out through the windows of the vehicle like Sesame Street's Oscar the Grouch hiding in his garbage can. She let go with a tirade of obscenities that managed to embarrass even a hardened old-timer like me.

Trooper Dow recognized Kaye (not her real name). Kaye was a rather obese young lady from town. She'd been arrested for operating under the influence a few times before. Not once did she ever go to jail peacefully. By the looks of it, tonight wasn't about to be an exception.

Trooper Walter Chapin had had the pleasure of dealing with her in the past, as she commenced to kick and destroy the inside of his police cruiser. She broke out the side window, and completely covered him with spit on the way to the lockup. She was a real beauty!

Bruce stated that he was well aware of Kaye and of her past history. She was capable of downing a barrel of booze all by herself, he claimed. "Whenever she does, she gets meaner than a raging bull in a rodeo," he added. It appeared as if she was maintaining that same old bitchy attitude tonight, by the looks of things.

I stood on the trunk of the car, directing a beam of light on her at all times. Trooper Lindahl positioned himself on a snow bank with his light shining directly into her face and his sidearm in the ready position. Trooper Dow was prying on the locked door with a tire iron, hoping to force it open. She was screaming and carrying on like a wild animal tethered in a small cage. The tension was quite high, to say the least. Kaye was wearing a pair of gray sweatpants and a pink sweater. Her hair was all messed up and she was incoherently babbling and screaming a tirade of threats against us all. It wasn't a very pretty sight, for sure.

Suddenly, Dave screamed, "She's getting the gun, Bruce! She's getting the gun, look out!"

At that same moment, the door popped open, allowing Bruce to reach inside and drag her out of the car and onto the snow-covered roadway. Dave later remarked about how close he had come to pulling the trigger in order to protect his fellow officer and those of us nearby.

Quickly grabbing the loaded shotgun, Bruce handed it over to me for safe keeping, as they fought with the struggling Kaye, who by now was sprawled out in the deep snow in the middle of the road. Bruce slapped the handcuffs around her wrists, demanding for her to stand up, which she flatly refused to do.

A quick check of her unconscious passenger revealed that he was no threat, as he remained in the car, completely oblivious to anything going on around him.

I slowly walked behind the troopers as they dragged Kaye, feet first, out through the snow-covered road and back to Dave's cruiser. I couldn't help noticing how her sweater had slid up to her neck, exposing her rather large, bare breasts. They were flopping and dragging along in the deep snow behind her. It was an embarrassing sight to witness, as I walked along listening to the foul-mouthed woman screaming nasty and intimidating threats at all of us. She refused to help herself in any way!

I couldn't help but chuckling however, looking at the marks her breasts had left in the deep snow. It looked like a skidder sporting Canadian chains had just traveled up the highway.

Dave offered to transport Kaye to the lockup while Bruce made arrangements to secure the car and transport the male passenger to a safe place for the evening. As we climbed into the cruiser, Kaye was still screeching obscenities and threatening us with bodily harm, if we didn't turn her loose.

She called Dave and me every foul-mouthed name imaginable, and even some I'd never heard. Then I saw a splat land beside me, as she began spitting in our direction— "lungers" as we call them in police lingo. The next few minutes were like trying to stay dry in a dunk tank at a carnival show, as we ducked and dodged the wet flying missiles that were sailing all around us. No amount of talking was about to persuade her to stop her actions. I even threatened to gag her with my used handkerchief if she didn't knock it off, but it didn't matter. She never heard a word I said.

"I have some great gangster friends in Boston and they'll see that you bastards pay for what you're doing to me," she screeched at the top of her lungs.

All of these threats were accompanied by another blast of endless name-calling and more flying lungers. It definitely was going to be a long ride to Belfast.

Making matters even worse, as we approached the town of Searsport, Dave pulled up behind another slow moving vehicle. This car was traveling from one side of the road to the other, indicating the driver was either highly intoxicated or he was having a medical issue. Then the vehicle began traveling directly down the center of the road, forcing oncoming traffic to take to the ditch in order to avoid a collision.

Dave said, "I've got to stop him, John. He's going to kill someone."

Stop him, he did! He too ended up being arrested for operating under the influence. With no other place to put him, the poor guy ended up in the back of the cruiser seated next to the screaming Kaye. Her continuing tantrums certainly sobered him up some quick as he never uttered a single word during the entire trip to the county slammer. Kaye began yelling and screaming at him too, but by then she was getting pretty well yelled out. No longer did she have the ambition or nasty desire to keep hollering or the capacity to keep spitting. Without a doubt, the well had gone dry!

Once at the jail, my buddy Dave escorted the male prisoner into the facility, leaving me alone to handle Kaye. By now she was bawling her eyes out and desperately begging for mercy. She pathetically pleaded for me to hoist her sweatpants back up around her waist, as they were hanging precariously low, exposing her backside. Feeling somewhat sorry for her sad state of affairs, I attempted to make her as presentable as possible before going into the jail. It was the least I could do. Struggling to reach completely around her for a good grip of the sweat pants, I desperately tried yanking her britches up over her mountainous posterior. The effort was just enough to cover the bare necessities, but not much more.

"Thank you! Thank you!" she sobbed.

"You're welcome!" I replied.

Meanwhile, Dave and several other officers from inside the jail were staring out the windows watching the entire fiasco. They were hysterically laughing as they watched my well-intended efforts, while I slowly escorted her toward the door. I knew I'd never hear the end of my display of compassion for the babbling Kaye, and I didn't.

Kaye was found guilty at a jury trial later on in the year. She was given a lengthy jail sentence for her actions. That jail sentence actually gave her plenty of time to lose a little weight and to sober up, which remarkably she did. A few years later she returned to society, where she has managed to straighten her life out and actually has become a model citizen.

Yes, 1976 was certainly off to a great start—with yet more fond memories for the diaries.

To this very day, whenever I see a skidder sporting Canadian chains running along in the deep snow, I instantly have flashbacks of Kaye being dragged up that snow-covered road in Winterport on that cold and wintery February night in 1976.

Get The Picture--Click-Click!

I don't know what it was about a few of these females who had a history of driving under the influence that made them show so much hate and discontent for the police officers who were only doing their jobs. But there were a couple of them who surely made our lives a little more interesting.

Like the incident with Kaye, another similar incident occurred with a lady by the name of Marguerite on Aug. 26, 1977. The evening began like any other one, with the exception that on this night my new boss, Sgt. Bill Allen, decided to ride along for the evening. His presence would give us both a chance to get better acquainted with each other.

We were heading out for the evening, hoping to capture a night hunter or two.

As we traveled the Waterville Road in Unity searching for a secluded area to work, we came up behind a slow-moving vehicle. The female operator appeared to be either having a medical emergency, or she was under the influence of booze, as the vehicle swayed wildly from one side of the highway to the other.

Bill calmly said, "I think she's drunker than a skunk, John. We'd better pull her over before she kills someone."

Initiating the blue lights and the siren, signaling for her to stop, she quickly skidded to an abrupt halt right in the middle of the road, forcing me to take evasive action to keep from running into her. I nearly drove my new boss's head into the windshield in the process.

Sauntering up to the driver's side of the vehicle, we asked the lady for her driver's license and the other pertinent information to identify this obviously incapacitated young lady.

"What the hell are you pestering me for?" she defiantly demanded, as she floundered around in the car while pretending to be looking for her license.

"Well ma'am, it appears as if you've had a few too many pops to be driving. We can't allow you to continue because you're going to hurt or kill someone if we do," Bill authoritatively stated.

He might just as well have been talking to himself, because she never heard a word he said, nor did she care.

"Oh you gawd-damned frigging cops! You're always pestering someone. Why to hell aren't you out there capturing the real criminals in the world and leaving me to hell alone!" she screeched at the top of her lungs.

"You need to step out of the car ma'am," Bill demanded.

She slowly opened the door, nearly plunging face first onto the pavement. I could tell from the tone of Bill's voice that his blood pressure was starting to rise—as was mine.

"Are you gonna arrest me, you S.O.B.s? You'd better, if you know what's good for you! And you'd better be putting those freaking handcuffs on me because I'm one mean and dangerous bitch," she screeched.

She didn't have to say any more to convince us that she was telling the truth. Marguerite had all she could do to stand up, as she bounced off the side of her car and staggered around to the back of the vehicle. She fell, stomach first, onto the ground, between the two vehicles.

Bill had requested a trooper to start our way to handle the highway offense and the prosecution of this so-called lady. Maine State Police Trooper Dennis Hayden, a new rookie officer who recently graduated from the Maine State Police Academy, was a short distance away. The young and eager cop was quick to volunteer his services. Most troopers were known to go well out of their way to remove a drunk driver from the highways. Capturing a drunk to them was like corralling a night hunter to us! In this case however, his response might have been something that Dennis would later regret!

After propping Marguerite back up onto her feet, she leaned up against the back of her vehicle, teetering from one side to the other, while screaming a barrage of insults and obscenities at both Bill and me. She certainly wasn't being any too lady-like! I thought to myself, "Welcome to Waldo County, Willy, a place where every night produces a new level of entertainment," as we patiently awaited the arrival of the state trooper. All the while we were trying to maintain some form of civility to Marguerite, while awaiting Dennis's arrival. But for the most part, the effort amounted to nothing more than an act of futility. We had no choice but to listen to the raunchy tirade of insults streaming from this highly polluted lady. She described in great detail what a violent and dangerous character she could be.

Much to our horror, she suddenly dropped her pants and commenced to relieve herself right in front of us. Modesty certainly wasn't on the top of her list as she continued screeching at us while conducting her private business. No amount of persuasion was about to calm her down. She was wilder than a raging bull in a china shop, ready to attack anyone at the drop of a hat.

Within minutes, Trooper Hayden arrived at the scene. Bill and I were quick to turn the matter over to him, seeing as where the driving offense was more in his bailiwick than it was ours. We definitely enjoy dealing with wildlife, but nothing as wild as what she was!

Dennis tried reasoning with Marguerite, but it too was a useless effort. Nothing short of a swift swat upside of her head with a solid 2x4 would've shut her up at that point. Even that might not have worked. She was ready to tackle the entire world and she continued demanding to be handcuffed.

The young trooper decided to oblige her, as he gently steered her onto the trunk of his cruiser, while removing his cuffs to snap around her scrawny wrists. His action infuriated her further, as she suddenly leaped up onto the trunk of his cruiser, wildly kicking and screaming. She was desperately trying to kick the antennae off from the trooper's cruiser. It took the three of us to physically restrain her to the trunk, while placing the cuffs around her small but wiry wrists. All the while, she kept kicking, and shouting a steady barrage of obscenities. Once we had physically wrestled her off the cruiser's trunk and back onto the ground, we forced her into the squad car.

Trying to attach the seat belt around her waist was yet another traumatic chore. It was like stuffing a ferocious fighting pig into a gunnysack. She continued swearing, kicking, spitting, and biting, as we finally secured the belt around her. This female pit bull exhibited a side of police work that few people ever have had the opportunity to observe. Thank God, they were rare instances!

Times like this had me wondering why to hell anyone would pursue this type of a career. Folks could display the worst of human nature at times. This was one of those times!

After finally securing Marguerite inside the cruiser, we asked the rookie trooper if he wanted us to accompany him to the county jail.

"Nah, I'm all set," Trooper Hayden bravely boasted, as he quickly climbed into his cruiser headed for the county slammer some 30 miles away.

After Dennis departed the area, heading for the county jail, Bill and I both chuckled over the events we'd suddenly found ourselves involved in. We continued along our way, searching for a place to work night hunters. A short time later, we overheard Trooper Hayden calling the sheriff's office for assistance with Marguerite. She'd all but devastated the inside of his cruiser, kicking at the side window and completely covering him in spit while she continued to taunt the young trooper in an attempt to entice him into assaulting her.

She was screaming, "You think you're so gawdamn smart, you *%&*#* pig," she shouted. "Did you know that while you're busy hauling me off to jail, your buddies are back at your house having sex with your wife?" she screeched. "You get the picture, don't you? Click–click," she grunted, while trying to imitate the clicking sounds of the shutter opening and closing on a camera.

Poor Dennis, it was bad enough he was forced to deal with her verbal abuse, but this was his first trip to the Waldo County Jail in Belfast and he wasn't quite sure how to get there. I knew exactly how he felt, having been through a similar ordeal earlier in my career. But when I searched for the jail, my prisoner seated alongside of me was extremely cooperative, although frustrated that I couldn't seem to find my destination. The Waldo County jail was hard to locate, as it was situated on a side street in the city of Belfast, and not well marked.

Eventually Dennis reached the sheriff's office, with an escort of deputies who had met him along the way.

Early that next morning, as Bill and I were finally returning home from an uneventful night underneath the stars, we met the rookie trooper as he was just returning from the county jail. Without so much as cracking a smile, Dennis bellowed, "Ford, if you ever call me to pick up another damned drunk, I'm going to go a thousand miles in the opposite direction just to stay clear of you." I assumed that he was joking, but with Dennis it was hard to tell.

Oh well, it was all in a night's work. There's one thing about this law enforcement profession, you never knew from one minute to another what was going to happen. I reckon it was anticipating that unknown that made my job so exciting.

Come to find out, this wasn't Marguerite's first run-in with the law after consuming more pops than she should have. A few weeks earlier, she'd been arrested for the same offense in the city of Waterville. In that case, she somehow managed to steal the cop's cruiser and speed away from him, only to crash it a short distance away.

Marguerite, like Kaye, surely was a beauty. In my one and only encounter with her, I definitely got that picture she talked about. Click–click!

So Much For Being Incognito

One cold mid-winter day in 1971, I decided to hike across Unity pond using the department-issued snowshoes I'd been allotted.

As the area's new "baby game warden," I was trying to impress the people I'd be dealing with. Besides, I loved snowshoeing as a youngster. Now I could do it whenever I wanted and I'd be getting paid! I had yet to receive the department-issued snowmobile that I was promised. Besides, I thought people are more apt to be impressed by seeing their new local warden sauntering on up to them on a pair of snowshoes, rather than riding on some mechanical machine.

The snow was extremely deep. But the crisp fresh air made maneuvering around the pond quite refreshing. There were a few fishermen scattered here and there out on the ice. I stopped to check their licenses and engage in a little friendly chit-chat. Many of them were amazed to see their new warden out on the lake on such a cold and frosty day.

At the farther end of the pond, I came across two young high school students who were enjoying their own day of fishing. They were snuggled in close to the bonfire they'd built along the shoreline while watching their ice traps on the ice in front of them. Introducing myself to both of them, I couldn't help but think back to the days when, like them, I too enjoyed my time ice fishing out in the fresh air.

After a little conversation, I inquired if they had their fishing licenses handy. Gary quickly produced his, but his buddy Jim, rather hesitantly, stated that he didn't need one yet. He claimed he wasn't of the legal age that required him to possess one. At first I didn't question his response, but there was something about his demeanor that indicated a little hint of nervousness.

Something that struck me as possibly indicating maybe a little deceit.

Long story short, Jimmy recently had turned 16, reaching the legal age requiring him to purchase a license, but as of yet he hadn't gone after the required permit. It certainly wasn't the crime of the century by any means. I could easily put myself in his position, reacting the same way if the shoe had been on the other foot.

I used my best judgment, issuing him a verbal warning, with a promise from the young teenager that he'd get a license the very first chance he could. His failure to have the permit wasn't in any way damaging the game fish. Besides, the darn things weren't biting! I took Jim for his word that he'd remedy the minor issue in the near future.

After briefly talking with Jim and Gary, and answering a few well-asked questions about my warden's career and how I came about getting it, I continued hiking up to the farther end of the lake where my cruiser was parked.

Departing the pond, I went to my friend, Jerry Mullen's house in Unity for a hot cup of coffee and a little break. Jerry was the new state trooper assigned to the area. We both were beginning our careers at the same time

I hadn't been at the Mullen residence for too long before Jim Ross and his cohort, Gary Parsons, came skidding into the trooper's dooryard. Arriving at the door, I noticed they were carrying my summons book.

Jim said, "We found your summons book laying out in the snow as we followed your tracks up across the pond. Apparently it fell out of your coat pocket!" he theorized. With a devious grin, he added with a chuckle, "I have to tell you, that if you'd given me a summons today, I don't know as if I'd be standing here with your summons book right now!"

I liked their attitude, and moreso, their honesty. Both of these young high school students inquired if they could occasionally ride along on patrol to see what the job was like.

They thought my job was something that maybe they too would like to pursue for a career. A great friendship and bond developed between us from that day forward.

I saw so much of myself, and my own desires to become a warden, in their unrelenting persistence to ride as often as they possibly could. Like them, I constantly pestered Warden Verne Walker, to do a ride-along whenever possible. Thankfully he allowed me that opportunity and now I felt these two young lads deserved the same.

Their assistance was invaluable to say the least. I could count on them for a variety of things as my career advanced and as they aged. The more they accompanied me on patrol the more they wanted to pursue the same career I was enjoying.

Jim Ross eventually achieved that stature by becoming a brand new "baby game warden" in the spring of 1978. It was indeed a proud day for Jim, as it was for me. I knew exactly how he felt as he struck out into the field on his own. The personal dedication and the countless hours Jim spent patrolling at my side reaped him the rewards of that same dream we both pursued as youngsters.

Upon completion of warden's school, Jim was assigned to the Skowhegan patrol, a short distance north of my area. We often met along our district lines, talking over old times and sharing information. On a few occasions we worked a variety of cases together.

It was during one of those discussions when Jim inquired if I'd like to work a special assignment with him during Memorial Day weekend. He planned to venture out into the back country of Spencer Pond, a remote area in the northern part of Somerset County. This popular fishing spot undoubtedly would be infiltrated with many fishermen during the three-day weekend. Jim felt there would be plenty of illegal activity to keep us both busy.

"We can go in plain clothes, fish along beside them while monitoring their activities and watch for those who don't play by the rules. No one from up this way would ever know you," Jim stated. "I've been hearing of some real serious over-the-limit fishing cases, not to mention the other violations that occur by those who ignore the laws within that area."

Always looking for a change of pace and a little action, I quickly jumped at the chance to explore an area of the state that I'd never been to before.

"Let's plan on leaving early Thursday afternoon, so we can select a prime campsite. A place where we can see what's going on around us. It should be a good time," Jim excitedly said.

It sounded like a great opportunity to be a little productive, plus it would be a nice get-away into an area of the state I'd never seen. The Memorial Day weekend weather forecast was calling for unseasonably warm weather so the fishermen should be out in full force. The plan was in place.

Thursday morning, we packed our gear into Jim's undercover vehicle, strapped the canoe on top of the roof carriers, and headed for Spencer Pond. The rough road leading into the campsite was no superhighway. We managed to rip the muffler off his vehicle on our way into the area where we planned to pitch our tent. You could have heard us coming from Portland, by the time we rolled into the campground, as the old cruiser slowly poked through the muddy passage.

Just as Jim had planned, we were the first to arrive in an area where most of these transient fishermen would soon be converging. The dam to Spencer Pond was off to our right, as we pitched the tent in a location that would be our home away from home for the next few days. Spencer Stream swiftly flowed past our campsite. We were in a very peaceful and relaxing place for sure! All alone, out in the wilderness, enjoying the beauty around us… for the time being, that is. Life was good!

State regulations forbid fishing from the Spencer Lake dam or in the eddy waters below it. We figured this forbidden area would be a great temptation for many of those fishermen who ventured up onto the dam, even though there were signs posted all around it indicating that it was a violation of the state rules.

Below the eddy, there was a small island with the current flowing around both sides of the small mass of dry land. If need be, we could always maneuver out onto the island to monitor the backside of the dam for any illegal activity that might be going on in the area of the eddy and the dam itself.

We spent most of that afternoon and the early evening scouting the area, trying to familiarize ourselves with the terrain and with those places we planned to work. That evening we kicked back, enjoyed a nice meal cooked over the campfire and relaxed in the wilderness. Life was good – just the way it should be!

Later that night, a steady flow of vehicles ventured into the campsite as we comfortably stayed in our tent and sleeping quarters, resting for the early morning excitement. We could hear the laughter and the clanging of beer cans and the consumption of other happy spirits from those having fun setting up their own campsites. Our little private camping area quickly filled up with many others who arrived well after darkness had settled in. All of them were anticipating a great weekend of good fishing and a little partying.

Little did they know two Maine game wardens were camping right next to them, ready to spring into action should they decide to ignore the laws of the land. Or so, we thought they didn't know!

Rising early the next morning, we crawled out of the tent, amazed to see several people already stirring about the campsite. The smell of bacon and eggs cooking on a camp stove filled the air.

I had just poured my first cup of coffee when someone yelled, "Hey, John Ford! What the hell are you doing way up here?"

Oh-oh, so much for being incognito!

Glancing at the tent below, I was shocked to see a group of young fellows from my hometown, young men with whom I'd experienced a case or two in court the previous fall. Steve, Perry, Beaver, and a whole group of their buddies had arrived in this remote area. All of them came way up here from my section of the state. They were typical young adults. But when it came to fish and game matters, they weren't always above board. For the most part, they were very sociable and quite likable. We definitely shared a mutual respect for one another.

I shouted, "For crying out loud, what the hell are the chances of my driving way up here only to have half the hoodlums from my hometown tagging along behind me?"

I could see the look of disgust on Jim's face when he realized that most of these young men were people that he knew too. Several of them he'd gone to school with!

To answer my neighbor's greetings, I sputtered, "Hey Steve, how you doing? I thought I'd take a little break and come up here to relax for a change. I'm trying to get away from you guys," I chuckled, passing the statement off as though I was joking.

"Sure you are, John! I don't suppose you're up here looking to catch somebody doing something wrong, are ya?" Steven rather sarcastically responded.

Within a matter of minutes, the entire campground was well aware of the fact that two Maine game wardens were now in among them. The chances of catching any of these fellows in the wrong were slim at best. Oh well, at the very least they were on notice that they needed to be above board in their weekend activities.

Before the weekend was over, we all gathered around the community campfire telling a few stories, sharing a few brews, and getting to know each other on a more personal level. We actually had a good time, even though the trip wasn't intended to be that way! These hellions weren't bad characters by any means. They simply were a group of young men out having a good time among friends, engaging in a lot of partying, and occasionally even partaking of a little fishing. Their supply of beer wasn't lacking, that's for sure.

Later that day, Jim and I decided to put the canoe into Spencer Stream for a short jaunt down river to view the happenings below us. There were tents scattered all along the river bank with people milling around everywhere. Some folks were fishing, while others were simply basking in the unseasonably warm climate.

On the return trip, Jim spotted a couple of fishermen floundering around up on the dam. "Looks like we got a little activity on the dam!" he anxiously said. "Let's put in on the island and watch them for a while."

"Sounds good to me," I said, as we slowly maneuvered the canoe upstream to the small island a few yards below the eddy, making sure to stay well out of sight from the men up on the dam.

We cautiously pulled up the canoe onto the island and slowly belly-crawled into the thick bushes, waiting to see if these men were enticed into fishing in the closed waters down behind the dam. We had a perfect view of the three men scurrying around the dam with their fish poles in their hands.

Jim and I huddled close together, lying flat on our stomachs in the thick brush, watching and waiting to see if the temptation for them to drop a line in the closed waters below the dam was just too much for them to stand. Suddenly, out of the corner of my eye and out through the thick bushes providing our cover, I noticed the bow of a canoe slowly approaching alongside of us.

I poked Jimmy, "Stay low, stay low, there's a canoe coming up beside us," I whispered, not wanting to be seen by someone who might be paddling up into the eddy to illegally fish it themselves.

We hunkered down in the bushes, watching as the bow of that canoe slowly inched its way toward us. Then I suddenly realized there was no one in the canoe. Making matters even worse, it was our canoe that was now floating freely in the current. Apparently it had washed away from the backside of the island, and was freely floating all by itself, farther and farther out into the deeper water of the stream, slowly heading for the eddy above.

"Damn, what the hell are we going to do now? If we don't catch it soon, we'll have no other choice but to swim out after it. Either that or we will be stuck on this island without a means of getting back to shore," I sputtered.

Rank has its privileges I reckon, when Jim sheepishly volunteered to be the delegated canoe retriever. He waded out into the cold stream and grabbed the canoe before it was too late. So much for that little surveillance plan! The entire weekend had thus far been nothing more than a total disaster as far as capturing that anticipated string of violators we both envisioned.

The fish weren't biting; the black flies had come out in droves causing an unbearable amount of discomfort; the muffler was missing from his car, making it sound like a tractor in a demolition derby; and everyone around the camping area knew who to hell we were. What else could possibly go wrong? That original plan of high hopes and good warden work had turned into nothing more than one major catastrophe after another.

We decided to leave early Sunday morning without issuing so much as a warning to any of the many patrons who had invaded this secluded spot.

Topping off the weekend, on our way back home we ended up assisting Warden Alan Later and several other wardens at the scene of a drowning in a nearby river. A young fellow was fly fishing in the stream wearing chest-high waders when he slipped on a wet rock and fell into a deep hole. His waders immediately filled with water, making it impossible for him to swim. This tragic incident sadly cost him his life, as he was quickly catapulted into the swift-flowing deeper water, unable to break free from the fast current that was pulling him along. Late in the afternoon, his body was finally recovered in front of his family and friends who had witnessed the tragedy. They had been solemnly standing by awaiting the recovery of their loved one.

All in all, this was a Memorial weekend that I'd never forget. It goes to show that in this line of work one has to expect the unexpected at all times. Advanced plans may sound good in theory, but they don't always work out the way one would like to think they would. This latest excursion was a perfect example!

The biggest lesson of all however, was the realization that one might think they can go somewhere incognito, only to find out that it truly is a small world. Invariably, there will be someone around who will recognize you. Over the years I've found that to be the case, not only in the state where we live, but throughout the world.

It is a small world out there! Jim and I found that out, on Memorial Day weekend, 1978.

Up The Creek Without a Paddle

Recalling my last memory, when Jim Ross and I were nearly marooned on a small island behind the dam of Spencer Lake while on a special assignment, made me think of a couple of my warden buddies who actually found themselves "up the creek without a paddle."

As I scan through the diaries, I find that I certainly never lacked for activity. Every day seemed to present a challenge of some sort. Not all of the catastrophes were of my own making. Many of my brother wardens, if they were to be honest, would be able to relate a series of their own catastrophes. We all had them!

The busy hunting season for wardens was just beginning at the opening of duck hunting season in October 1981.

I hated working duck hunters. Every time I attempted the task with a sense of dutiful vigor, some major catastrophe always occurred.

I seldom came close to bagging a duck hunter for any major violations. More often than not, I'd find myself caught in the middle of some fiasco not worthy of the effort put into attempting to enforce the duck hunting laws.

I'm sure my above comment will get me a few negative comments from those members of the prestigious Ducks Unlimited organization and other waterfowl groups within our state, but sadly it is what it is, and that was the case for this warden anyway. I'd much rather have been chasing night hunters, as those violators were well aware of their crimes, even if it did take more time and patience to capture them. Not to say duck hunters aren't worthy of the same enforcement. They are! And obviously my duties required enforcing all of the rules and regulations. I couldn't simply pick and choose which ones I was actively pursuing.

That old saying of being "up the creek without a paddle" actually happened to a couple of my brother wardens on the late afternoon of Oct. 3, 1981.

Wardens Bill Pidgeon and Doug Tibbetts decided to sneak out onto Carlton Bog in the town of Troy in an all-out effort to bag a few duck hunters violating the rules, and do a little duck hunting themselves.

This large boggy area was located in the middle of my patrol area. The fact that other wardens were working within my patrol area was of no concern of mine. I never engaged in those territorial turf struggles that some of the other wardens seemed to maintain. There was plenty of activity to keep us all busy. Bill was an avid duck hunter and Doug always enjoyed sharing a day out on the bog hunting with his working partner. So I was tickled to death that they found my area to be enticing to work in for their own enforcement efforts.

Launching their boat at Carlton Bog, they were sporting the usual hunting garb, portraying themselves to be regular duck hunting enthusiasts and not the enforcement officers they were. They'd spend the afternoon bagging a few ducks of their own, while keeping a watchful eye on the other hunters in the area. Carlton Bog is a large boggy area. It is extremely well known for a variety of waterfowl. The bog is actually a part of the Moosehorn refuge, a desolate area of wetland situated between the towns of Troy and Detroit, with a small stream running full length down through the middle of the swampy marsh—typical habitat for all types of waterfowl. Most of the bog was situated within my assigned patrol area and was a favorite location for many duck hunting enthusiasts.

Later in the evening of Oct. 3, I was en route to Unity to meet my working partner Norman Gilbert for our regular rendezvous to seek out those dastardly night hunters. Darkness was settling in as I slowly headed for the location where we had planned to meet.

Content in my own little world, I cruised along viewing the countryside I was passing through, I heard Warden Tibbetts muttering on the warden's channel of my state radio, "Help! Help! Is there anyone out there? Hell-o! H-e-l-l-o! Anyone out there?"

His mumblings obviously didn't sound like a very serious distress call, but more like a call of sheer frustration from a lack of responses.

I quickly replied, "What's up, Doug? Are you all set?"

Doug anxiously responded, "Uh, yeah. We need a little help here, John. Is there any chance you can grab your boat and bring it up to Carlton Bog? We are stranded up at the far end of the bog, unable to move," he disgustedly grumbled.

"I'll be en route shortly," I informed him. I could only wonder what catastrophe was preventing them from moving.

Within minutes of Doug's radio traffic, I met up with a highly agitated Warden Gilbert, "What the hell is that all about?" he disgustedly sputtered.

Norman was extremely disgruntled with the two bordering wardens. In his opinion they had once again committed the cardinal sin of sneaking into another warden's district without letting that warden know of their intentions.

Personally, I could care less. I was happy to know that someone was willing to tackle the dreaded chore of working duck hunters in my area, thus saving me the effort. After all, we were in the same business. It really wasn't as if we had designated borders that had a "no trespassing" sign posted around it. The warden's badge said, "State of Maine" and wasn't limited to any specially designated area!

But Norman obviously did care, and he wasn't about to let it go.

He sputtered, "To hell with them. I think we ought to leave them up there! They've got no damned business going into your district without telling you." He was dead serious!

The fact that both Bill and Doug had previously tormented my poor working partner by sneaking into his territory and jokingly advising folks that he'd recently retired and now they were taking over his district, didn't help their cause any, especially during this time of real need for assistance.

After their little practical joke, Norman's phone was ringing off the hook with people wishing him well in his retirement. He was forced to explain their devious actions, as he adamantly advised folks that he was not retiring now, nor was he planning to in the near future.

Needless to say, the old boy wasn't any too happy! Bill and Doug were practical jokers, but by the same token, they both were damn good wardens. Most of us took their actions in stride, always expecting the unexpected whenever they were near. But in Norman's case, their deviltry had become a real personal bone of contention. A serious one at that.

"We can't just leave them there," I said.

"To hell we can't," he responded. "It will teach them a damned good lesson." He was as serious as I'd ever seen the old boy.

Eventually, I was able to persuade my partner that we should go to their rescue, which we did. But not without Norman voicing his total disgust and disdain for the two wardens who suddenly found themselves in a rather precarious situation.

As darkness settled in at the bog and the last group of hunters departed the area, Bill and Doug decided they'd accomplished their mission for the day. Bill started the boat engine, only to find out that he had neglected to firmly secure the motor to the boat's stern. The motor quickly spun free from the boat, plunging into the water behind them. As if that wasn't bad enough, they suddenly realized in their haste to get onto the bog, they'd forgotten to bring paddles.

For them, that old adage of being up the creek without a paddle was a reality.

Doug managed to find a small board floating in the grass and weeds. He attempted to use it as a paddle, but for every 20 feet he went forward, the wind blew them 25 feet backwards. In other words, they were going nowhere!

Thus on that cold dark night of Oct. 3, 1981, under the cover of darkness, Warden Gilbert and I came to their rescue as we slowly towed our cold and hungry co-workers down the stream of Carlton Bog and back to their parked cruiser.

All the while Norman sat firmly perched in the front of the boat, disgustedly scowling and staring at the two brother wardens as we slowly headed for the boat landing. The silence was golden!

He stared at them like an angry father, ready to take his two sons to the woodshed for a well-deserved whipping. Norman was not a happy camper and the boys obviously recognized this fact as they humbly held onto the tow rope for the slow journey through the bog. If the old boy had his way, they'd still be there!

I simply smirked at the obvious tension. In essence I was pleased to know that I wasn't the only warden to ever work duck hunters who occasionally ending up in a mess.

As an active member of the dive team, Bill spent the next day retrieving the outboard motor from the bottom of the bog. This time, he and Doug brought paddles for the boat and all the necessary equipment to get to and from the area.

As for Norman, well let's put it this way—he didn't offer to help them in any way.

This was yet another fond memory for the diaries, one which to this day still brings a smile to my face. Searches and water rescues were among the many tasks we wardens were often called upon to perform, but seldom did we get the call to rescue our own.

In the meantime, thinking of my pals Bill and Doug stranded in the dark, in a boat up the creek of Carlton Bog without a paddle really "quacks" me up! (Pun intended!)

Norman on the other hand—well what could I say? It was rather obvious what he thought!

Working With The Pidgeon

Thinking about Wardens Tibbetts and Pidgeon brings back memories of when a change of supervisors in 1972 found me working with a new partner for the fall season. For whatever the reasons might have been, I no longer would be partnered with Norman Gilbert. Instead, I'd be working with Warden Bill Pidgeon of Plymouth.

Bill was very outgoing and he had a personality that was second to none. I'd become rather accustomed to working with my old partner, Norman, so to now be paired up with someone new was a bit different to say the least.

It was hard changing the work habits one had become accustomed to, and this change in working partners certainly created a new working environment. I guess I'd been spoiled in that working relationship I'd been in for the previous two years. Norman was more laid back and Bill was much more hyper, energetic, and certainly more playful!

That fact became evident on one of the very first nights we patrolled the area together as a team. We had decided to use his vehicle, working in an area that he was very familiar with.

He said, "Bring your sleeping bag with you. I prefer lying outside of the cruiser, listening to what's happening and going on around us. You miss a lot by sitting inside the car with the heater running, you know."

He was absolutely right. I knew there were times when probably Norman and I had missed hearing shots off in the distance because we were chatting inside the car while the heater was running full blast. Not that it would have made any difference had we heard the shots; chasing them always proved to be fruitless.

On this particular night we were parked in an area well known for night-hunting activity. It was an extremely dark, cold, and frosty night. The stars overhead were shining brightly. It was cold enough to see your breath in the night air.

Bill exited the car, quickly gathering up his sleeping bag and neatly spreading it out over the hood on his side of the vehicle. Following suit, I grabbed mine and did the same thing over on my side of his cruiser. In no time, Bill was snuggled comfortably inside his sleeping bag, as I climbed up onto the hood and quickly crawled into mine.

I'd no more than settled into the garment, when I began sliding down across the hood, rapidly picking up speed along the way. I slid off from the vehicle, landing in a big heap onto the ground in front of the cruiser, much to the hysterical delight of my new partner.

I soon discovered that Bill had waxed my side of the hood earlier in the day, knowing damn well what the end results would be. He'd purposely set me up in one of his playful moods! It was nice to know that I'd provided him with a chuckle or two.

I simply filed this little harmless prank away in my mind, hoping to initiate my own form of retaliation later on. There's an old saying that we hear quite often, "Payback is a bitch!"

For the remainder of that night, I found myself sprawled out up on the roof of Bill's cruiser, listening to my new partner snoring away below me.

That was Bill. I realized that whenever I was around him, I needed to expect the unexpected. And usually he didn't disappoint me. On the other hand, working with a new partner was proving to be quite productive as far as picking up our share of night time violators. Together we were having a banner year. Actually, we were leading the division in the number of night time apprehensions. At least we were doing something right, and we were having fun at it. I anxiously looked forward to working every night, wondering just what kind of excitement the night would bring.

Late in the evening of Nov. 24, 1972, we apprehended a group of three rather intoxicated night hunters in the town of Dixmont.

They were a little uncooperative at first, but after confiscating their two loaded rifles and informing them that they'd be going to the Penobscot County Jail, they soon calmed down and became a little more cooperative. Bill offered to accompany one of the violators and bring his car to the county jail in Bangor. His name was Perry. I took custody of the other two in the cruiser, following behind Bill and Perry for the long ride to the Bangor lockup. This little arrangement was more of a convenience to them. One so that they'd have a means of transportation from the county lockup once they'd posted the appropriate bail to guarantee their appearance in court.

We began the trip to Bangor with Bill seated on the passenger's side of Perry's vehicle that poked along in front of us. I was close behind, trying to make small talk with my exceptionally quiet prisoners. Suddenly, I observed through the glare of my headlights shining into Perry's car, Perry falling over in the seat and completely disappearing. The car started swinging wildly from one side of the road to the other.

Bill was frantically thrashing around inside of the vehicle in an obvious attempt to regain control of the situation. They shot off the road and down into a grassy ditch, screeching to an abrupt halt in a big cloud of dust. Thankfully, they weren't traveling too fast and were in an area where there were no large objects to collide with.

Apparently, Perry had suffered an epileptic seizure and passed out without any warning. His condition may have been triggered by the excitement of the moment. I'd certainly been there and seen that horror show before. A young fellow once had a similar attack in the backseat of my cruiser while I was issuing him a citation for fishing without a license! Having never seen such a sight, I was sure my detainee had died during that long trip at warp speed to the doctor's office in Unity. But that was then and, this was now!

I skidded to a sudden stop just as Bill jumped out of the car. "Jeezum, jeezum, jeezum!" he was yelling.

Bill was about as excited as I'd ever seen him. He was shaking like a dog passing razor blades.

"Perry's just had some type of a gawdamned seizure, but I think he's coming around," Bill nervously shouted.

By then, Perry was standing outside the vehicle vomiting. It was a scene of mass confusion and chaos, so typical of how quickly situations can change in this line of business.

"Gawdamn it," Bill shouted after everyone calmed down and had regained their composure. "I'm driving the rest of the way," he sputtered, as he bluntly ordered his prisoner back into the vehicle for the remaining trip to the county jail.

Bill slid in behind the wheel, backed hastily out of the ditch, and shot off down the road like he was trying to set a land-speed record. I had all I could do to keep up with them. Within no time we were booking our guests into the Penobscot County Jail.

Upon departing the jail, Bill said, "I don't know about you, John boy, but I'm ready for a gawdamned drink!"

Reaching into the trunk of his cruiser, he pulled out a couple of civilian shirts that he conveniently had stashed away, just for such an occasion. The next thing I knew we were seated at a little bar somewhere down on Hancock Street in downtown Bangor, soothing our nerves and celebrating our night's hard work with a drink or two. I sensed from the warm personal greeting Bill received when we entered the place, that it wasn't his first time there.

Yup, working with Bill was a lot different than working with Norm. After all, the only thing I ever saw Norman drink was warm cow's milk—and plenty of it! I really did miss the old bugger and his ways of doing business. Personally, for whatever the reasons, I wasn't quite as comfortable with this sudden change in working partners. I certainly wasn't the least bit at ease spending any amount of time at a bar in Bangor, when we should have been out working. But due to the unusual circumstances of this particular evening, I figured perhaps Bill may have needed a little break. For now, anyways!

A few nights later, we apprehended two more night hunters, this time in East Newport. These deer-slaying murderers were operating a small foreign car equipped with a sliding sun roof. The driver was intent on lighting the fields with a high-powered spotlight, while the passenger stood up through the sunroof toting a loaded 30-06 rifle. He was ready to kill anything they saw. They never knew we were following them driving without headlights as they shot and killed a small deer grazing in an old grown-up field.

You can only imagine the shocked and surprised look on their faces when the quiet night air was suddenly shattered with bright lights and the screaming siren of our cruiser. The hunter peeking out through the sun roof in the small car, suddenly disappeared inside the vehicle like a woodchuck diving into his hole for safe cover.

You talk about getting caught with your hand in the cookie jar! This offense was yet another trip back to Bangor and to the county jail. Once these violators were booked and processed, Bill wanted to return to the little bar back down on Hancock Street, but this time I refused. I was extremely uncomfortable the first time we'd visited the little joint, and I wasn't about to make a habit out of bar-hopping in Bangor every time we picked up a bunch of night hunters.

Making The Best of It

As previously noted, the 1972 hunting season was not quite as normal for Norman and me, especially with each of us having new working partners to contend with. We'd grown accustomed to our own mode of operation and suddenly it all had changed.

Norman was assigned to work with Warden Doug Tibbetts from Corinna. Doug and I were hired by the department within a week of each other.

Ironically, as I was completing my Air Force career, stationed in the good old state of Maine at Charleston Hill, Doug and I were next-door neighbors, living in a small Kenduskeag trailer park off the airbase.

Doug was employed at a plant in Bangor at the time. We often shared our hopes of one day becoming game wardens, while having a beer together. Amazingly, we both realized those dreams and attended the 1971 warden school together. Raising a fair amount of hell, both in and out of class, seemed to be natural with a friend like Doug. It helped having a classmate you were somewhat familiar with.

Actually, after school one evening, the two of us rather innocently were involved in an incident that damn near got us fired by the bosses. But that's another story—one that just might not be told!

After a brief stint patrolling in Aroostook County, Doug moved to the Corinna area. That first week Doug assumed his new duties as a Maine game warden in Aroostook County, he and Warden Charlie Merrill were involved in a high-speed chase with a couple of night hunters. The passenger in the offending vehicle decided to lean out the window with a rifle, firing random shots at the wardens pursuing them. One of the bullets blew the mirror off of Doug's side of the cruiser, an act of violence that surely got his full attention.

The chase eventually ended without anyone being hurt, but the circumstances of that night showed just how dangerous this profession could become in a moment's notice. These poaching subjects all had serious criminal records and were notorious for their defiance against the law and cops in general. Their little episode with the wardens got them a fairly extended stay at the state's crowbar hotel.

Doug was a loud, boisterous fellow and a lot of fun to be around. But he was just a little too active for Norman's sake. By the same token, it was no secret that Doug opted to be with his old working partner, Bill Pidgeon. I guess there was no appeasing "Grampy" but it was obvious he preferred the old way of doing things.

Doug and Bill had worked well together. It was obvious that they too were not all that happy with the changes in working partners and habits. If there was one common trait among wardens, it was the fact that we all hated and resisted a change in operations. This new change in working conditions happened to be one of those times.

Doug and Bill constantly tantalized poor Norman, accusing him of being too old for the job, or they chastised him for the jug of milk he depended upon to fix his ulcer. But then again, we all teased him about his habit of guzzling warm milk during those so-called times of stress. It was all in fun, until one day they seriously crossed the line, riling the old fella up about as bad as I'd ever seen him.

Bill and Doug decided to work in Norman's district while he was resting at home taking his usual afternoon nap, right in the middle of the deer hunting season. Norman was extremely protective of his district and he especially didn't want anyone working it without getting his permission first. If there was something going on in his area, he deserved to be made aware of it.

Bill and Doug, realizing how touchy Norman was about others imposing on his private little domain, decided to raise a little harmless hell. It didn't matter to either of them that they had entered sacred territory. Together they encroached upon one of Norman's deer tagging stations.

In their conversation with the agents at the little country store they were asked, "Where's Norman?"

Bill boldly stated, "The old fella has suddenly retired, and we've been assigned to take over his district." Bill told this fib knowing damn well that word would quickly get back to Norman. Which it did!

In the meantime, the rumor that he'd suddenly retired spread like wild fire throughout Norman's district. Their little harmless fib managed to push the old boy over the edge. He scurried throughout his district trying to re-establish his foothold into that sacred territory that he called his own.

He wasn't long venting his anger toward the boys in a way that everyone within the agency was quite aware of. There was fire shooting out of both eyes and steam coming from his nostrils, as he desperately searched for the culprits who spread such a rumor.

When all was said and done, Doug and Bill knew they'd seriously crossed the line with the old bugger, and that it was going to be a long time for them to get back into his good graces. If they ever did! Not that they really seemed to care.

Bill fessed up to being the main culprit in spreading the vicious rumor. He did so with a big smile! Norman made it very clear that he wasn't about to forget the uncalled-for prank and he managed to emphasize that fact quite well a little later with poor Bill paying the price.

Where Are You, Bill?

It was a late October evening when Bill and I were working night hunters in a remote area in the town of Troy.

The fall rain came down in buckets on this rather cold night as I backed the cruiser into a woods road overlooking some old apple trees and small clearings. This location was well noted for being heavily frequented by deer.

Bill was wearing a heavy jacket and his rain suit. He figured it might be worth his while to spend a little time perched down along the roadside, making sure that anyone passing through the area got a glimpse of what looked to be deer eyes in their headlights. This little act of deceit was a method Bill used, one which seemed to be working pretty well.

If anything was to happen, I was to scoot onto the main road without using any lights and he'd simply jump inside the cruiser and we'd make the stop together well away from the area. I simply figured, what the hell, if he wants to sit outside in the rain with his hood up and his rain jacket on, trying to entice someone into seeing a deer, that's fine by me. I planned on staying inside the car where it was warm and dry.

It wasn't long before the headlights of an approaching vehicle slowly came our way. Suddenly, the vehicle came to an abrupt stop right near the apple trees across the road from where I was parked. A bright beam of light began sweeping the area searching for those eyes of a deer feeding underneath the apple trees. Not finding any deer, the vehicle slowly proceeded on down the road.

Night hunters, I thought, as my heart started pounding and the adrenaline started flowing, just like it did every time we were about to make a stop for the illegal act. By then, it was pouring cats and dogs outside, as I quickly maneuvered the cruiser into the roadway, waiting for Bill to jump inside.

No Bill! I waited and waited and still no Bill.

The offending vehicle by now was pulling farther and farther away. If we didn't get going, it would be gone and we'd have lost that continuity needed to prove our case. With still no signs of my partner I figured he must be sleeping on the stone wall or something. I made a command decision and shot off down the road in pursuit of this violator before he escaped altogether. I ended up in a small chase of sorts that ended when the vehicle I was pursuing skidded to a sudden and rather abrupt stop.

As I reached the side of the vehicle I saw the hand-held spotlight lying on the front seat, along with a loaded .30-30 rifle beside it. This was all of the evidence I needed to prove my case. I had no choice but to arrest Jerry, and haul him off to the Waldo County slammer, some 35 miles away.

"What the hell are you doing out on a miserable night like this, John?" Jerry sheepishly asked.

"Well, Jerry, maybe I should be asking you the same thing," I responded.

I knew Jerry quite well, recalling an incident just a few days earlier when he'd pulled the wool over our eyes in regards to another incident involving a little deer poaching. Needless to say, I was a bit excited to have him humbly seated alongside of me, knowing that what goes around comes around.

Still, I was wondering where Bill was, and moreso, what he must be thinking. I certainly couldn't go back to pick him up, now that I had a prisoner seated beside me. I didn't want Jerry to realize that Bill might have been part of the reason he'd committed the act of night hunting.

Along the way to the county jail some 30 miles away, I contacted Norman on the radio explaining Bill's predicament for being left behind. I knew that Norman and Doug would figure out what Bill was doing.

Explaining exactly where Bill was left in the freezing rain, and with no means of transportation, I all but begged Norman and Doug to go pick him up.

"No, gawdamn way. He's made his bed! Now let him lie in it!" the stubborn old duffer sputtered. It was obvious Norman wasn't about to rescue Bill, and I knew Doug would have little to say about it! Knowing Norman as well as I did, I could just envision that sly but devious little smirk on his face, as he was personally enjoying every minute of Bill's misery.

I made the trip to the Waldo County jail as rapidly as I possibly could without scaring the be-jeezus out of my prisoner. All the while I was thinking about poor Bill, stuck out in the rain and the bitter cold without a place to go for shelter.

It was a couple of hours before I finally returned to where I'd last seen my partner. I wondered if he was still there.

I'd no more than pulled into the woods road when the door was ripped open and a half-frozen and highly irritated Bill quickly jumped inside. His head was bobbing up and down like one of them damned old bobble-head dolls that people firmly plant in the back windows of their cars. He tried yelling at me, but all he could do was stutter. He was shivering and shaking uncontrollably, obviously feeling the effects of the cold elements outside.

"Jeezus – jeezus," he shouted. "I was just reaching for the #*!&%*# door handle of your car when you shot away like a rocket, leaving me standing there," he angrily grumbled. "Why to hell …" he never did finish his remarks, as his head was uncontrollably bobbing up and down and he was shivering too badly to carry on with any conversation whatsoever.

A small part of me really felt sorry for what had happened, but yet another devious part of me was somewhat amused, as I thought back to the night he waxed the hood of his cruiser and to other practical jokes he'd been pulling on me from day one.

I recalled that old saying, "Payback is a bitch!" Although it wasn't purposely planned, I believe that a subtle, inadvertent form of payback had definitely been meted out.

"Take me home," Bill angrily demanded. Those were the last words he uttered for the remainder of the night.

For the rest of the trip to his house, he just stared straight ahead, all humped up, shivering and shaking like a little puppy in dire distress.

Oh well, at least we'd captured another night hunter for the stats. We certainly were having a very productive fall, especially compared to that first year when Norman and I hardly spun a thread, as we patiently watched and waited night after night for a night hunter to come our way. That first hunting season we just heard those occasional rifle shots off in the distance, knowing full well that we were perched in the wrong place!

Bill may have been a pain in the arse of sorts, but we surely were having great success and accomplishing our goal of apprehending night hunters. The fact that we were having such good luck really irritated Norman. This working night after night after night, hoping to apprehend violators was always quite competitive between teams!

If you are fortunate enough to be in on the action, it's fun. But if you're not, it makes for a long and boring night. From my personal point of view, I was still having more fun and doing a job I enjoyed. It just didn't seem like work. I couldn't imagine doing anything else with my life.

Not every day in the life of being a game warden do things go exactly as planned or as well as we hoped they would. There were those times when some catastrophe or some blotched effort in a well-thought-out plan occurred—and then there were times when something out of the ordinary happened.

The following story is one example of those times.

The Great Pheasant Catastrophe

In the early 1970s, the department was heavily involved in a statewide pheasant stocking program. The purpose was to promote the bird-hunting season, along with an effort to sell the required pheasant stamps to hunters engaging in the activity.

One of the central locations for this stocking program was the Frye Mountain Game Management area, which was part of my patrol area. Frye Mountain Game Management area consisted of more than 5,000 acres. It was owned and maintained by the Fish and Game Department. It was located in the Waldo County towns of Knox and Montville, and had been purchased by the state solely as a place for sportsmen of Maine to enjoy all kinds of recreational activities—priorities being the hunting season in the fall, the hiking season in the summer, and snowmobiling access and trails in the winter.

The department hoped to draw the state's bird hunting crowd to the management area by releasing 200 pheasant each week during the bird hunting season. The plan was to scatter them across the mountain in what was known as a "put and take program." It was similar to the statewide fish stocking program, wherein the department released several brook trout raised in its fish hatcheries, into ponds and streams around the state, solely to appease fishermen. The "put and take program" was the agency's attempt to lure sportsmen into buying a fishing license with a guarantee of catching fish in return.

The same was true with the pheasant program—a pheasant hunting stamp was required to possess any of these upland game birds, with the hopes of giving the hunter and his dogs the thrill of a hunt. These types of programs were intended to increase the sales of hunting and fishing licenses, which were the main sources of funding for the department's operations.

Most of the management area consisted of grown-up farmlands and fields—perfect habitat for upland game birds, including those pheasants we released on a regular basis. The area provided a popular spot for hunters and their trained bird dogs during the fall hunting season. It was a great place to enjoy a day's hunt, often with very successful results.

The pheasants released on a weekly basis were independently raised by local growers over the course of the summer, strictly for the purpose of enhancing the sport. The department encouraged various sporting groups and clubs to take on the project of raising the birds. In turn, they were given the eggs and a small amount of monies to help with the effort.

Late every Friday afternoon during hunting season, 200 pheasants were crammed into small wooden crates and delivered to a storage shed at the entrance of the management area. There, they were readied to be released and scattered over the mountain at the end of the day's hunt. We wardens often accompanied biologists who strategically placed the birds across the mountain in anticipation of the upcoming week's hunt. Usually this activity was accomplished late Friday afternoon, shortly after legal hunting time, in order to give the birds a chance to spread out before the influx of hunters from across the state arrived early the next morning.

It was a "put and take" program for sure, as the birds seldom strayed from where they were released. In one aspect it promoted the state-owned land by giving the bird hunters a chance to watch their bird dogs perform, while providing the hunter with a meal in the process.

One particular fall afternoon, a freelance writer was assigned by the main office to accompany us on our little excursion as we released a bunch of birds for the upcoming hunt the next morning. His plan called for taking several photos of us in action as we sent the birds aloft. Afterward, he would write a well-structured article for the popular *Field and Stream* magazine, detailing the entire event, and praising and promoting the area and the department's efforts. His inclusion into this day's activities was an all-out effort by the fish and game department to promote and publicize the pheasant-stocking program and to show its great success.

It was a hot Indian summer afternoon when he arrived for his photo shoot. The temperatures were unusually high that day, compared to what they normally were for that time of year.

We met at the little outbuilding at the entrance to the mountain, where earlier in the day the packed crates of pheasants had been neatly stacked on top of each other, ready for the late afternoon release. They were properly stored in the back of a pickup truck, awaiting that moment to distribute them out into the many fields up on top of the mountain.

With a small convoy of vehicles heading up over the narrow road we stopped at the first set of fields. It was show and tell time. Time to open the crates, allowing the birds to fly away to a new freedom!

The photographer, kneeling in the tall grass, was armed with his expensive camera and big lenses that he had aimed at the back of the truck. He was hoping to capture the birds' flight of freedom on film, as the biologist opened the doors on the small crates and released the birds into the wild.

Instead of the normal mass exodus of flying pheasants, most of them simply fell out of the crates completely motionless onto the ground. They were either dead or near death. Apparently they'd suffocated from having been packed into such tight quarters in the extreme heat. Out of the entire flock, only a few birds were capable of flying away, and even those required a little tender loving care before shipping them off into the wilderness.

The shocked look on our faces must have been priceless—the entire episode was captured on film by our tag-along reporter. I quickly recalled my old buddy, Maine State Trooper Mark Nickerson's wise advice, "You always want to deny pictures!" But unfortunately, there was no denying this catastrophe!

Oh well, sometimes things don't always go as planned. This was one of those times.

The generous gift of a couple of fresh birds for the reporter's grill helped persuade him to delay his story for yet another day, a day when hopefully the situation would be better managed and far more productive. Thank God he took the bribe, sparing the department the embarrassment it deserved.

That was the last time the pheasants were ever left stacked on top of each other. It was a lesson well learned!

I'll Be Right Out

At the beginning of my young career, I found myself working both day and night from the late summer on through the end of the hunting season. I certainly wasn't the only warden in the state doing it—we all did. "Burning the candle from both ends" was the term my bosses used to refer to the long hours worked.

Did I happen to mention how the deer hunting season in my area seemingly started on the Fourth of July when the first batch of peas were ready, and it didn't end until the second blizzard hit the area in late December?

I thoroughly enjoyed the prospect of working those dastardly night hunters, especially anticipating those hair-raising, adrenaline-filled moments attempting to make an apprehension once the dirty deed had been committed. There was something special about the self-induced testosterone rush that came with the chase that was just unexplainable. It was like a euphoric high that seemingly lasted for hours!

I never regarded the 100 or more hours a week as remotely being work. How could I? I was definitely living the professional career I'd longed for, so how could I possibly call it "work"?

There was an old adage floating around stating, "If you had a job that you really loved, you'd never work a day in your life." I certainly could vouch for the fact that truer words were never spoken. Sometimes though, working long and tedious hours had its drawbacks, especially when fatigue and total exhaustion ruled the moment.

I recall one of those times when I was suffering from a serious lack of much-needed sleep and it resulted in an incident when I became a total embarrassment to a young state trooper I'd recently befriended. My lack of a response to a situation he was involved in had to have been a great disappointment for the young lawman.

Trooper Richard Phippen of Vassalboro was en route to the town of Newport at 2 a.m. to assist members of his agency with an investigation of an armed robbery that had just occurred. As he and several other troopers sped toward the scene, Dick decided to take the back roads of Burnham, hoping to possibly meet the culprits involved in the robbery meandering around out in the back country.

As he slowly cruised across the rural Johnson Flat Road in Burnham, Trooper Phippen observed a vehicle exiting an old grown-up field. Curious as to what they were up to at that early morning hour, the young trooper signaled for them to stop along the narrow dirt road.

As he cautiously approached the vehicle, he observed what appeared to be fresh blood on the rear bumper of the car. These young men were extremely nervous and very evasive regarding the questions being asked of them by the young state trooper. The unloaded firearm on the floorboards of the vehicle suggested the group might possibly have been doing a little night hunting. After all, what other reason was there to be out in an old field at that particular time of the morning.

Being somewhat unfamiliar with the operational procedures of the fish and game rules, Dick assumed he didn't have the authority to force them to open the trunk or to arrest them for a night hunting violation without having seen them committing the dastardly act in person. But he suspected there might be a dead deer in their trunk.

Trooper Phippen requested the state police dispatchers to call my residence, advising me of the situation and the circumstances surrounding it. He offered to stand by the scene awaiting my arrival and to assist with any search if I felt it was warranted.

I'd just crawled into the comforts of my warm bed a short time before, totally exhausted from the days and hours of running around without sleep—burning that candle from both ends! I was thoroughly encased in that deep sleep I so desperately needed. The past two days of working continuously, running from one complaint to another, while attempting to do the necessary follow-up investigations had finally taken its toll.

The loud ringing of the nearby telephone suddenly jolted me awake from that sound deep sleep I was enjoying.

"Hello!" I groggily responded.

"Warden Ford, this is the state police barracks in Augusta calling. Our trooper, Richard Phippen, has a vehicle stopped on the Johnson Flat Road in the town of Burnham with several young men in it. They are in possession of a firearm and they have what appears to be fresh blood on the trunk. He believes they possibly might be night hunting. He wanted you advised," they stated. "He is assisting other officers in an armed robbery in Newport, but says he'll detain the vehicle until you arrive, if you're interested. Shall I tell him you'll be en route?" the dispatcher inquired.

Suddenly my eyes snapped wide open, as I mentally pictured the scene. It sounded like the perfect chance to hold some of these night-hunting critters accountable for their dastardly deeds. To be handed a bunch of these bandits as easily as this was a great gift indeed. After all, they were the very reason I found myself spending countless nights parked in some old remote field to begin with. They certainly needed to be held accountable for their sins and this young trooper deserved the credit.

It appeared as if Dick had all the evidence needed to develop a good case for court, cinching it with the possibility of even having a deer in the trunk.

"Interested! Interested! Does a bear poop in the woods? You're damn right I'm interested," I excitedly told the dispatcher.

All the while I was desperately trying to force myself awake. "You advise him I'll be right out and I'll meet him at the scene," I informed the dispatcher

I overheard the radio conversation with Trooper Phippen as they relayed my response. I barely remember glancing at my watch, noting that it was just a little after 2 a.m. The next thing I remember was waking up at 8:30 in the morning, with my uniform pants half on and half off. There I was sprawled out across the couch, half-dressed and wondering where the heck I was, and moreso, what was going on? Suddenly, I remembered the phone call from the state police some six hours earlier.

In my haste to respond to Dick's request, I started to put on my uniform pants and that was as far as I got. Completely exhausted, I apparently twirled around and flopped back down on my couch, where I quickly dropped off into a sound sleep once again.

Now several hours later, as I sat there rubbing my eyes, I vaguely recalled the conversation, wondering if perhaps I'd just dreamed about the early morning call or if, in fact, it had really happened. If it wasn't a dream, I imagined that trooper Phippen was madder than a dog chewing razor blades. And I couldn't blame him.

I quickly dialed the state police headquarters.

"Augusta State Police, may I help you?" a voice calmly responded.

"Hi!" I said, "This is Warden Ford in Burnham, my call number is 807. Look, I seem to vaguely remember getting a phone call earlier this morning from your station, something to do with your trooper Phippen stopping a car in Burnham with deer hair and blood on the trunk and a group of young fellas toting a rifle inside. Can you tell me if he is still there?"

With a snicker, the female dispatcher said, "Nope John, he signed off at home a few hours ago. He said if you called, for us to tell you to disregard meeting up with him. He gave up waiting for you and turned them lose after sitting there for an hour and a half!" Sarcastically, she inquired, "Did you go back to sleep, John?"

"I guess I must have," I stuttered, as by now I realized this wasn't a bad dream after all.

"I don't wonder!" she sympathetically stated, "All of us have been wondering when to hell you guys ever sleep. It seems as if you are on the radio in the morning, during the day, and then all through the night! How to heck do you guys do it?"

"Dedication, ma'am! Nothing but pure dedication," I humbly said. "Thank you for your time," I said, as I hung the phone back up.

I sat there on my couch, my pants still half on and half off, sulking and thinking of how I'd probably just missed a golden opportunity to bring some of those damned old diehard Burnhamites to justice for night hunting. I was thoroughly disgusted with myself for the lack of effort. It was completely unacceptable to let such a golden opportunity slip by, especially to have me sprawled out on my couch trying to get a little more shut-eye rather than responding to such a great opportunity.

A few days later I met up with my newly found trooper buddy and desperately apologized for my sins.

"I kinda wondered what the hell was taking you so long," he disgustedly stated. "Finally I said to hell with it, figuring that you weren't coming out. So I cut them loose."

Dick then handed me a list of names of those he'd confronted. I launched into a tirade of cuss words I'd never dare print, as I read down through the list of names. I recognized every one of them. They were notorious throughout the area and were well known for their poaching activities. I'd spent countless hours trying to catch them in the act of committing their dastardly deeds. All to no avail.

When the opportunity finally presented itself, where to hell was I? Curled up between the sheets, counting sheep, and snoring like an old Partner chainsaw. Not much I could do about it now. Hopefully there would be another time and another place.

One thing for sure, time was on my side. Whether trooper Phippen ever would be again or not, I had my doubts! Like the old saying goes, "You win a few, and you lose a few!" This time the bad guys got the break.

That issue of sleep, or the serious lack thereof, certainly had taken its toll on this young rookie. That's what you get for thinking you can burn the candle from both ends. Eventually the effort catches up with you. This was one of those times when it did!

Planes, Trains, and Games

Late in the evening of Oct. 12, 1978, Norman and I were again working night hunters in the Burnham area. We were secured in a place known for having an abundance of deer, near an area where the Maine Central Railroad tracks separated a couple of large green fields. The trains hauled car loads of freight and wood from Dexter to Waterville daily, with the route of travel directly through this location, usually under the cover of darkness.

On this particular cold and frosty night, we were huddled inside the cruiser, patiently watching for a dastardly night hunter to venture our way. It was exceptionally quiet outside, with very little traffic cruising through the area. Off in the distance, we could hear the train coming from Pittsfield, as it clanged and banged along the iron rails, rails that eventually would bring the large beast directly behind us.

As the train approached the fields, we noticed it appeared to be traveling exceptionally slow. The bright lights from the engine illuminated the entire area, including the surrounding fields.

Suddenly, a rifle shot rang out, drowning out the noise of the slow moving train. We simply assumed someone was poaching on foot out in the back field beyond the tracks.

Exiting the cruiser, we quickly headed for the area where the shot appeared to have come from. It seemed rather ironic that the train suddenly picked up speed after it passed those remote fields.

"Norman, I think that shot might have come from the train," I whispered, as we cautiously scanned the back fields for any signs of activity.

"I think you're right. We need to work on that, John boy," my partner said.

Earlier in the month, I'd captured a local railroad employee and one of his cronies for night hunting. Upon seizing the evidence, I noticed the hand-held light they were using belonged to the railroad. Could it be, this man might be hunting from the train, too?

The next day, we contacted railroad security, advising them of our suspicions. I told them about capturing one of their employees who had been using railroad equipment to night hunt. Upon naming that individual, I was advised that the man was assigned to the Dover/Waterville route and that he definitely would have been working on the train the night we heard the shot.

The railroad detectives encouraged us to do whatever was necessary to put an end to these shenanigans, even if it meant boarding and impounding the train should those on board be observed committing a violation. Apparently, this employee had been a major problem for them in the past few years. They were more than cooperative in helping us attempt to bring him to justice, with the hopes that in the long run it might resolve their own issues.

"Would you mind if we climbed aboard the train and traveled along the route, hoping to catch these guys in action?" I inquired.

"Hell no, go for it!" the agent replied. "Like I said before, if you can catch them in the act, we only ask that you impound the train and don't let it go anywhere. You contact us, and we'll come right up and take over from there. The train's daily route of travel comes down the line from Dexter, stopping for just a couple of minutes in Newport while they switch onto the tracks for the run south into Waterville. If you want a place to jump aboard, that's it!" he advised. "Get as close to the caboose as you can, that's where your man will be," he chuckled.

With their blessings, we implemented a great plan of action. We planned to hop the train, riding it from Newport to Waterville. Sgt. Bill Allen enthusiastically joined me on the first run. This was a new way of working night hunters, while at the same time giving us a little excitement to boot! The plan called for Norman to drop us off in Newport. We'd hide in the bushes and wait for the train to arrive. While it switched lines, Bill and I would scale up onto one of the boxcars closest to the caboose. From there we could hunker down for the long, cool ride south. Norman would be following along out on the highway, maintaining constant contact with us on the portable radio should we need help.

I advised Bill, "I think we can jump off in Fairfield when the train slows down as it travels through town. Norman can pick us up there!" All things considered, it sounded like we had the perfect plan.

It was show-and-tell time, when on Oct. 19, 1978, Norman dropped us off beside the tracks in Newport. We hid in the nearby bushes, patiently waiting for the train to arrive.

Right on schedule, we heard it coming our way. Chug, chug, chug, clankety-bang, clankety-bang, the metal wheels ground on the iron rails as it came closer and closer to our location. My heart was pounding like a race horse in the Kentucky Derby, knowing that we only had a few minutes to accomplish our goal. It was show time!

Soon the big mechanical monster came within view, screeching to a halt directly in front of us. Satisfied that the coast was clear, we quickly scrambled out of the bushes and up onto a rail car three cars away from the caboose. It was the perfect location to observe the caboose and its occupants. The boxcar was loaded with pulpwood. The metal ladder attached to the side of the rail car made it easy to climb to the top.

We perched belly down on the very top of the woodpile, listening to the shuffling of feet and voices below us as the crew went back to the caboose, completely unaware that we were only a few feet above them, monitoring their every move.

Within minutes, we were rolling along the rails, headed for Fairfield. It was a brutally cold night. I found myself shivering uncontrollably. I think I was shivering more from the sheer excitement of the moment than I was from the cold.

In no time we were sailing down the tracks in total darkness, rocking back and forth like a baby in a cradle. Once we were well away from town, we tossed off a couple of pulp logs in order to make a small shelter out of the wind, and in the pile of wood surrounding us. Actually, it was quite cozy and comfortable.

I couldn't believe how fast we were traveling, as we shot away from Newport, down through Detroit and into the town of Pittsfield. Clickety-bang, clickety-bang—the big train squealed and rocked along the iron rails.

Looking out over the wood pile, we observed the men inside the caboose sitting around a small table. They surely appeared to be a hell of lot warmer than us. But I bet they weren't having as much fun.

Leaving Pittsfield, I said, "We're coming into the area where they shot the other night, Bill, so we might want to be ready!"

My heart was really pounding. The adrenaline was starting to pump into my veins, like a blood transfusion. If they happened to shoot again, the plan was to wait until the train stopped, and then make our presence known, rather than busting down the door in the caboose while sailing along the narrow rails. I recall performing that task on another train episode earlier in my career, and it wasn't exactly what I called a good plan of action. You learn from your experiences, I reckon!

Disappointingly, we sailed straight on past those fields without ever slowing down. Nothing like what the train had done the week before.

Within minutes, we pulled into Burnham village, where the train made yet another stop. Lying motionless on top of the rail car, we once again heard the men talking and walking around us, unaware of our presence. The workers shifted a few cars from one rail to another, in the rail yard located along Route 100 in Burnham. In no time, we were once again underway.

I told Bill, "There's some big green fields coming up as we head into Clinton. Maybe they'll take a shot there," I disgustedly grumbled. I was quite disappointed that nothing had happened yet.

In no time, we were sailing along at the same high rate of speed as before, as we cruised through Burnham and into the town of Clinton. As we entered Clinton, I leaned over the side of the rail car, trying to see what was going on inside the caboose.

Suddenly I was startled by a loud whoosh – whoosh – whoosh – whoosh passing my head by mere inches. Several empty boxcars parked adjacent to the rails that we were on extended almost out to where we were. There was little room to spare. "This is a good way to get decapitated," I thought to myself, as I quickly pulled my head back, like a snapping turtle retreating into its shell.

We whistled straight on through Clinton and into Benton. The next town coming up was Fairfield. By then it was obvious we weren't going to make any big bust on this night, as we'd already traveled through the prime deer country with nothing out of the ordinary happening.

Bill moved down onto the ladder at the end of the pulp car we were riding, preparing to bail from the train as it slowed passing through Fairfield village. He was a couple of steps below me, hanging onto the metal ladder of the rail car as we violently swayed back and forth.

I was climbing down to join him, when suddenly I noticed just how high up in the air we were as we sailed out over the waters of the Kennebec River, with the water glistening in the moonlight far below us. My fear of heights suddenly took over. I had a death grip on that metal ladder that a stick of dynamite couldn't have removed. I'd forgotten all about that damned old river and the narrow railroad bridge crossing above it.

It really didn't matter though. Before I could really think any more about it, we'd crossed the river, but we didn't seem to be slowing down as much as I'd planned for, as we came to the railroad crossings in the middle of downtown Fairfield. The train whistle was blaring away and the signal lights were flashing, with Bill and I securely attached to the ladder on the road side of the railroad car.

We shot straight on through town nearly as fast as what we'd traveled from Newport. There was no way in the hinges of hell that we could have safely jumped off that train in Fairfield Village as planned. We obviously were along for the ride into the nearby Waterville rail yard, if in fact the train stopped there. We clambered back up to the woodpile and disappeared out of sight.

Within minutes, the train slowed as it entered the yard in Waterville, allowing us the opportunity to safely jump away. Eventually, we met up with Norman just outside of the train station, where we happily basked in the warm and welcome heat in his cruiser. It had been a damn cold journey via the rails.

Sadly, our suspects didn't cooperate that night. There would be another time and other nights. This wouldn't be the last of the Newport-to-Waterville excursions by any means.

I was kind of disappointed knowing that my hopes of advising the state police barracks that Bill and I had just impounded 36 railroad cars, two engines, a caboose, and the entire crew of the Maine Central Railroad, were all for naught! Maybe the next time around our luck would change!

Warden Lowell Thomas joined forces for yet a couple more trips south on the MCR, but just like before, we never had that exciting success we'd hoped for. Come to find out, our suspect was out on sick leave with a bad case of the flu. When he eventually returned to work, the engineer that he was in cahoots with went away on a vacation. Thus, our little game plan was placed on hold for the time being!

Being in the right place at the right time never did materialize. But it was the excitement and the dedicated effort that we put into it that I'd always remember. The failure to bag the MCR poachers certainly wasn't because we didn't try!

This job certainly had its moments of excitement. The train rides from Newport to Waterville happened to be among the top. Stay tuned for when the nighttime "spy-in-the-sky" makes its initial debut—one that provided yet more memories and excitement for the diaries. It was going to be an interesting fall for sure.

The Spy in the Sky

The year 1978 marked a new era for trying new adventures in law enforcement techniques within the Maine Warden Service. Even with the increase of penalties and fines, accompanied by a mandatory jail sentence and loss of equipment, night hunting remained a major concern throughout the state.

In the fall of 1978, the warden service experimented by utilizing the department's aircraft to fly under the cover of darkness and watch and observe activity on the ground in an attempt to recognize and apprehend poachers from the air.

Warden Pilot Dana Toothaker was in charge of the operation. He was assisted nightly by another warden who acted as an additional navigator and spotter. Between the two of them, they'd guide the district wardens on the ground into areas where it appeared illegal activity was being observed from high overhead.

On the first night of this new operation, my working partner, Norman Gilbert, was acting as Dana's navigator. The added eyes high above were a great assistance to those of us on the ground. While we were restricted to watching just one specific area, they could cover miles from up above.

I'd no more than taken up surveillance in my little hiding spot when Dana stated, "You've got a vehicle riding through several fields on a remote back road near the Troy/Dixmont line. You might want to head that way to check them out!" he suggested.

Immediately I headed in that direction while Dana and Norman circled high overhead keeping tabs on the vehicle.

Dana was directing me into the area. "Douse your lights so they won't see you coming," he instructed. "You're almost up to where they're at!"

Doing as he suggested, I was slowly traveling over the familiar dirt road without using my lights, anticipating the possibility of apprehending someone attempting to jack a deer using their headlights. Norman and I had apprehended night hunters in this same location in the past, so the possibilities were good. It was a typical bright moonlit night, allowing me to easily travel along without headlights.

"They're down in the back of that big field where you're at and off to your right," Dana advised, as I slowly turned into the field.

Within moments, I fell in behind a pickup truck slowly cruising the edge of the large green field. They didn't have a clue I was there, until I snapped on the blue lights signaling for them to stop for inspection. My heart was pounding and a steady flow of adrenaline was rushing into my veins as I anticipated that sense of fight or flight that so often accompanies this type of activity.

Much to my disappointment, I found three young men searching the area with a coon dog riding in a strike cage protruding from the front of their truck. The hound in the strike cage would alert the driver if it picked up the fresh scent of a raccoon. The remaining dogs would then be released, pursuing the coon through the woods, eventually treeing it for the sportsmen to shoot.

This type of nighttime activity was perfectly legal, as long as the hunters didn't possess a high-powered rifle or any other instruments associated with the act of night hunting. A 22-caliber pistol was perfectly legal and was more than enough firepower for a coon hunter to bag his quarry.

I was quite familiar with these young hunters. I checked their licenses while casually talking with them, being cautious not to reveal how I'd learned of their presence so far away from civilization.

They didn't have a clue the "spy in the sky" was circling high overhead without the use of lights. I could hear the drone of the plane above, but the boys never thought a thing about it.

I quickly departed the area, advising Dana and Norman that they were coon hunters, perfectly legal in their activities. Before the night ended, I checked this same bunch of coon hunters two more times. Each time they were in another place, quite some distance from where I'd checked them before. Dana had me scurrying from one area to another, with high hopes of bagging night hunters, only to find the same crew of coon hunters.

During my first confrontation with these amicable sports, they assumed I had wandered onto them routinely.

The second time around, they questioned if perhaps the department wasn't now using an aircraft to find them. They casually mentioned hearing the drone of the small plane engine that seemed to be circling high overhead. I half-heartedly denied using the plane, not wanting to alert the sporting community of this newest enforcement technique that we were now utilizing.

But when I confronted them the third time, they were quick to let me know, "Bullshit you're not using an airplane, John! Now you tell us just how coincidental it is that every time you suddenly appear, there's a guy up there in the sky circling around?"

I could only shrug my shoulders and walk away. I knew before long, word would travel throughout hunting land that we wardens had gone high-tech, airborne to be exact, in our aggressive pursuit of those dastardly night hunters. Oh well, what the heck. If nothing else, this newest sky-high adventure broke up the monotony of sitting in one place all night, patiently watching and waiting for a night hunter to come along, while listening to shots off in the distance and wondering if perhaps we shouldn't move.

In the early morning hours of this first night's test run by Dana and my working partner, the radio crackled once again. Dana inquired, "Are you still in Troy?"

"I am. I'm parked just off from the North Dixmont Road," I said.

"We're going to call it a night," Dana suggested. "We're quite a ways south of you right now. Is there any chance we could meet up with you at the Pittsfield airport in 10 minutes or more?" he inquired.

"Sure thing," I stated. "It'll be travel time from here. Probably about 15-20 minutes," I advised them.

By now, I was half asleep as I headed for the Pittsfield air strip. I couldn't wait to get home for some much-needed sleep. I slowly drove out onto the dirt road where I had been parked, heading for Pittsfield a few miles away.

The North Dixmont Road was in a rural area along the top of a hill. It was surrounded by several large fields, several old apple trees, and very few houses. The area was well known for its abundance of deer.

As I cruised along the ridge of this narrow dirt road, I was fighting to keep my eyes open. Fatigue was definitely setting in. I couldn't wait to slide between the sheets of a nice warm bed. The music was loudly blaring on my car radio as I drove along in the dark of night, heading for that rendezvous with Dana and Norman.

I was just passing an area where the power lines crossed the highway, winding their way down through the woods and out across the countryside. Off to the right side of the road there was an old grown-up apple orchard that surrounded the power lines. That orchard and the apples on the ground were a great draw for the deer in the area. As such, there were a few tree stands located in among the area where hunters had bagged a big buck or two in the past.

As I cruised along in a minor trance of sorts, I was suddenly startled by a loud roaring noise overhead. The entire area was completely illuminated by fast-moving, extremely bright blinking lights.

I thought I was under attack by a *Star Wars* space ship. That damn duo of Dana and Norman had deviously decided to play a prank on yours truly. Flying in the black of night they were directly over me when they decided to dive bomb my cruiser.

At a point just a few feet overhead, Dana snapped on every light in the plane and throttled up the engine to full throttle in order to streak back up into the air like they had just made a bombing run. The noise alone was deafening and the lights were bright, to say the least! Their actions scared the ever-loving be-jeesus out of me. I wasn't so sure but what my Fruit of the Looms might need to be discarded! Needless to say, I certainly wasn't as sleepy as I'd been. The boys got me, and they got me good.

But the story didn't end there. A few weeks later, rumors were circulating throughout the area concerning "those crazy freaking wardens."

Apparently a certain individual, living not too far from those power lines and the old orchard, was illegally seated in one of those tree stands during those same wee hours of the morning, waiting to bag a deer of his own. He was what we wardens called a foot-jacker.

Dana's diving plane was directly over him as well. The sudden intrusion from outer space, caused him to jump out of his tree stand, spraining his ankle in the chaotic spur of the moment.

"Those *#! damn fools are nuts," he relayed to his buddies the next day. I certainly couldn't argue with him on that point.

Perhaps that early morning incident by the department's kamikaze pilot, and that low-level run over the North Dixmont Road might just make an old poacher give up his illegal activities. But I knew better, and so did he. Old habits are hard to break—and he had them bad! I was sure of one thing, I bet he became a lot more cautious than ever before.

If he's reading this story today, as he very well could be, for the first time he'll know that I did hear of his fall from grace that early morning due to the outer space alien attack.

Ah, there's nothing like the satisfaction and a little poetic justice from someone who deserved the turmoil. Maybe, just maybe, another huge Troy buck was saved from the perils of a bright light and a rifle shot.

All of this happening in a long night's work underneath the twinkling stars of the heavens. An interesting night at that.

The Beginning of a New Era

Lt. Charles Tobie

Several personnel and operational changes were occurring within the department during the late 1970s. Some of them were for the good and, in my opinion, many others were not.

A slew of the older wardens were retiring—wardens who had left their individual legacies within the warden service and especially great memories for some of us younger employees who were in need of a little leadership, me being one of them!

My boss, Lt. Charles Tobie, came to the realization that it was time for him to step aside and enjoy his own private life, as he too retired just prior to the 1978 fall hunting season. The unexpected move by the boss brought an end to his long and productive career. Charlie was a great boss to work for. I often wondered if perhaps it wasn't some of my actions that might have prompted him into suddenly deciding to pull the plug.

Take for instance, my first year with the agency. One late fall afternoon Charlie discovered my state-issued boat had been left totally unattended for weeks, parked near the woods in my dooryard. I'd neglected to remove the drain plug as it sat on the trailer behind the warden's camp that I called home. Needless to say, the boat nearly filled to the seats with water from heavy fall rains.

Charlie pulled into my dooryard to inspect the watercraft one afternoon while I was out on patrol. He found a 14-foot block of solid ice. Obviously, as the boss, he wasn't any too happy. Nor should he have been.

Charlie was a real stickler when it came to caring for the department's equipment. Admittedly, I on the other hand, was completely opposite in that aspect. It seemed like I was always rushing from one detail to another, never taking time in the interim to properly care for my issued equipment. It was a damn poor excuse on my part, but this was just one of the many bad habits I unconsciously seemed to operate under.

The day Charlie noticed the condition of my backyard ice-boat and brought it to my attention, I was totally unaware of its condition. I'd never given the watercraft a thought as I went about my normal duties.

During a radio conversation between us, he rather sarcastically inquired, "John, I'm here at your house. Is there any chance I might be able to use your boat to go duck hunting?"

Being far away, I responded, "Sure, it's in my backyard. Just grab it and go," I replied, never expecting there might be a problem!

Disgustedly, he screamed into the radio, "Have you even looked at it lately?"

"Why would I want to look at it? What possibly could have changed since I placed it there earlier in the fall?" I silently pondered to myself, as I held the radio microphone in my hand.

Charlie then demanded that I meet him at my residence, immediately! I could tell from that grumpy tone of his voice that he wasn't happy. I soon found out exactly what the issue was. His feet were barely touching the ground as I pulled my cruiser in behind the Burnham warden's camp.

"You take this goddamn boat to a heated garage somewhere, and you thaw it out," he angrily demanded. "And that doesn't mean if I drive by here in an hour or so, that I want to see you standing inside of it, chopping it out with a goddamn chisel," he screamed.

Defining that was a wise move on his part, because the very thought of doing just that was certainly on my mind.

Charlie was as angry as I'd ever seen him—justifiably so I might add! He departed my dooryard in a fit of disgust, spinning rocks and dirt all over the dooryard.

I knew right then and there that I was in deep do-do. At this point in time, there was nothing I could do to rectify my errors. For what seemed like hours, I tried hoisting that 14-foot block of solid ice off the ground in order to connect it to my cruiser, so I could tow it over to a friend's heated garage. Accomplishing this task was a hell of a lot easier said than done! I noticed the boss didn't bother hanging around to help in any way. As angry as he was, I was damned glad he didn't.

Thank God for my handy-man jack and a whole lot of patience. I finally managed to hit the right combo, as the trailer hitch fell onto the ball, nearly lifting the front end of my cruiser up off the ground. Eventually I managed to get the department's "ice boat" to a friend's garage, where in time it thawed out, hardly none the worse for the circumstances it was in.

Another incident that really got Charlie's panties in a knot, occurred one day after the boss had attempted several times to contact me on the radio, all to no avail. I'd neglected to sign out of the cruiser as per the department's protocol. Instead I was off poking around the woods in Knox, looking for illegal traps. Jim Ross and Warden Lowell Thomas tagged along for company. We actually had found a few!

Occasionally, in our haste to accomplish some task outside of the cruiser and away from the radio, we would exit our cruisers, failing to notify the state police barracks of where we were or what we were doing. In the meantime, if they were looking for us we simply were unavailable. Such was the case on this day. But on this day, it was the boss who wanted me, and he wanted me right then! When we finally met, he was just as wild as an old sow bear with a real bad attitude.

"Where to hell have you been, and why didn't you sign off the radio like you are supposed to? What if we needed to get in touch with you in a hurry?" he angrily inquired.

I responded with the typical response I normally used whenever I didn't have a good logical explanation for my actions. "I dunno. I forgot, I guess!" I humbly mumbled.

Obviously, my response did little to satisfy the master. I managed to receive in front of Jim and Lowell, one of the worst butt-chewings ever from the boss.

When Charlie finally finished chewing on my ears, we ended up going to a local diner for lunch. As I humbly walked through the front door with Lowell, Jim, and Charlie tagging along close behind, he was still ranting and raving about my not following the required radio protocol. Once we were comfortably seated inside the little restaurant, and when it appeared Charlie's feet were back on solid ground, I couldn't resist asking, "Did you sign us off with the barracks so they'll know where we are, Charlie?"

I knew damn well he hadn't. Indirectly I was sending the boss a subtle little message of my own. One that was kind of like "what's good for the goose is good for the gander!"

Great gobs of guppy-poop, that certainly wasn't one of the brightest moves I'd ever made in my career. If looks could have killed, I'd have been dead right on the spot!

"I'll gladly discuss this afterward if you really want to continue with the conversation, John!" he defiantly sputtered, staring at me with daggers coming out of his eyes.

"Nope, I'm all set I guess," I humbly stuttered, wondering why to hell I'd made such a stupid remark in the first place.

I noticed a silly smirk on Lowell's face. He knew that I'd just infuriated the boss even more than he had been. As my career advanced, I didn't have to wonder why I never climbed up that ladder of success within the agency. By far, I was my own worst enemy—and I knew it!

Another minor confrontation occurred between us a little later on, after Warden Thomas and I spent most of the day cutting up and packaging meat from an illegally killed moose that had been shot in Lowell's area.

Together, we feverishly cut, sliced, and wrapped meat all day long at a friend's butcher shop in Montville. We gave most of the meat to several informants throughout our area, people who really could use it and folks who had helped us in the past. This act of kindness was our way of saying "thank you for your great support." Without the help of the public, a game warden was fighting an endless battle of sheer frustration. Giving salvaged game meat to those who helped us throughout the years was a common practice statewide by just about every game warden. It was good public relations that usually paid big dividends.

We never worried about the liability issues such as government meat inspections or the accountability back in those days, as sadly has become the case today. Coddling the public was good relations—and what better way to obtain a sense of cooperation than to reward them whenever we could. Personally, I didn't care about moose meat and Mrs. Ford didn't like the smell of it cooking.

Whether Charlie thought we'd kept the meat for ourselves or what, I could only guess that he did. A few days later, he bluntly inquired, "What ever happened to all of that moose meat you guys cut up the other day?"

I commenced to tell him what we'd done with it. Obviously, he was not too overly impressed when he demanded that Lowell and I revisit all of those folks who we gave the meat to, and have them sign a receipt for every package of meat they'd received. Up until now, such a requirement had never been mandated or even heard of.

Lowell, a more seasoned warden than myself, sputtered, "I'll be damned if I'm going back to those people, asking them to sign one damned thing! If Charlie wants to go visit them on his own, he can. No one's ever been required to do this before, and I'll be damned if I'm going to now," he defiantly muttered.

Lowell, like me, was noted for having an independent streak of his own.

Long story short, neither of us ever attempted to provide the list of names the boss had asked for. Defiance and independence seemed to be traits we wardens possessed. There were times when we dug in our heels, taking a stand on issues that we didn't believe in. This situation happened to be one of them.

Lowell said, "For us to have to do that might make our supporters think that we could be posting their names for the public to see. These folks demand total anonymity in their contacts with us. Suddenly asking them to sign receipts for a few packages of moose meat might just jeopardize that anonymity, resulting in a lack of trust from those very folks we depend upon the most. I just ain't doing it."

"Well if you're not going to, than neither am I! What the hell are they going to do, fire the both of us?" I bravely asserted.

We never did attempt to gather any of those receipts as the lieutenant requested. The matter was occasionally a topic of conversation, but it never got enforced.

Now that the lieutenant was retiring, I couldn't help but wonder if perhaps these combined acts of rebellious incidents may have been just enough disgruntlement to push Charlie over the edge. But I really didn't think so. There were several issues occurring within the agency far more serious than ours for the boss to deal with. Without a doubt, many of the new operational changes within the organization forced Charlie to recognize that his time had come, along with those of several other old-time wardens.

Little did I know it at the time, but a few years later I'd find myself in the same boat and for the same reasons. We all seemed to realize when enough was enough—and when it came time for us to pull the plug, we did it.

Charlie had a very productive career. He deserved to be rewarded for his efforts. I, for one, would miss his many chats, the overall friendship, and the great support, even though at times we were at odds with each other. I kind of enjoyed tantalizing him to a certain degree. As a boss, he was doing exactly what he was supposed to. I deserved the brunt of his wrath whenever I got it.

As I stated earlier, Charlie prided himself in caring for the department-issued equipment that had been assigned to him, far more than most of the wardens in the field. On his final journey to the storehouse to return his issued gear, he had one of his most-prized possessions in the trunk of his car. It was an old outboard motor that he'd kept in immaculate condition over the many years he had it in his possession. To see it, one would think it was a brand new piece of equipment. Charlie cared for that outboard motor like it was his own little baby during all those years it was in his care.

Upon returning his gear to the storehouse, he had placed the shiny motor in the storehouse parking lot fairly close to his cruiser as he continued unloading the rest of his assigned gear from the cruiser's trunk. Eventually, the motor was destined to find its way inside the building for safe storage.

On that day, there were several wardens who were coming and going from the storehouse, all of them making comments of praise regarding the excellent condition of the old outboard motor in the parking lot. Hearing those complimentary comments, Charlie beamed with pride. They were definitely good for his ego.

Before day's end however, John Marsh, the new lieutenant for the division, had to go somewhere in a hurry. In typical John Marsh fashion, he jumped into his cruiser, quickly backing around in the large paved parking lot at the storehouse, readying for a trip out onto the main drag. There was a large bang, followed by the grinding of metal upon metal.

Exiting his cruiser to see what the cause of all this noise was, the new lieutenant discovered Charlie's outboard motor was firmly stuck underneath his cruiser, smashed into a gazillion pieces. In a matter of a few seconds, John had completely destroyed Charlie's pride and joy!

Needless to say, the "old boss" was not highly impressed with the "new boss!"

Retirement

On Sept. 8, 1978, wardens from all over the state gathered for a banquet honoring Charlie for his well-deserved retirement. Charlie was certainly going to be missed by those of us who knew and worked for him. After all, he was from the old school, and he was used to doing things the old way. We all worked together as a team, getting the job done without having so many restrictions being placed upon our work ethics, methods, habits, or the long hours we worked.

As a gag, I couldn't resist to send one more subtle message to the boss as he sat before us for the last time. I had created and framed a scratch board drawing of a bull moose, with a large roll of toilet paper hanging from its antlers, and a list of several people's names neatly penciled upon it.

This list supposedly represented that list of names of those informants who Lowell and I had given packaged moose meat to a few months earlier. The last two names on the list were written in large bold letters. They were Lowell's name and mine. We both were sure that he was of the impression we had kept most of that moose meat for ourselves.

In that cool, calm, and collected Tobie style, he politely smiled, while at the same time giving me that look of discontent that I'd seen so many times before. I just couldn't resist winking and smiling back.

Scratch board drawing presented to retired Lt. Charles Tobie

New Direction - New Leadership

With the recent retirement of Lt. Tobie, Lt. John Marsh assumed the reins as our newest leader. He did so with great enthusiasm.

John was intent on sending a message to the sportsmen of Maine that the warden service was very much alive and well. For many of us, it would be the beginning of a new era.

John quickly initiated several new enforcement techniques during the fall, hoping to initiate a better means of apprehending more of those night hunters who were threatening our deer herd. The new fines and penalties still had not curtailed the activity as it should have. The night hunting was just as rampant now as it was before.

One method of curtailing the activity was using the department's aircraft to fly under the cover of darkness. The hope was to capture these nimrods in the act, as I wrote about in an earlier story in this book. That extra set of eyes, along with the ability to cover a much larger area, were great assets to those of us sitting stationary in the field. The midnight "spy in the sky" definitely brought a few great memories for the diaries. This unprecedented effort was just one of many ideas that the new lieutenant was contemplating.

There was no doubt the times were drastically changing for all of law enforcement, including our agency. In my opinion, 1978 was the start of a new era for the warden service. The days of old were being guided by new blood with bold ideas. Several updated changes in work habits and techniques were being implemented every time we turned around. Some of those changes were for the best, while others left a little something to be desired.

Amazingly, I already had eight years in the history books, with 12 more to go! In that short period of time I'd seen several changes in procedures and staffing. I witnessed the retirements of several old bosses and friends. The time was flying by much faster than I ever could have imagined. The memories were piling up in record form, and the job I loved was still an answer to my prayers. It was just as much fun after eight years as it was when I first started. Who could ask for anything more?

The Pine Tree Hitching Post

During my years patrolling in the Unity area, it seemed as though there was a constant turnover of Maine State Police troopers assigned to the region. It seemed as though I'd just become well acquainted with one of them, when he'd either move up the ladder of success within his agency after a promotion, or in some cases simply resign, or in one case he was fired.

It was in the late 1970s when Dick Reitchel, another new trooper fresh out of the State Police Academy, was assigned to the Unity area. Dick and I immediately formed a great friendship. It was as though we'd known each other for years. I found myself spending countless hours patrolling with Dick, showing him around and introducing him to the many folks I knew. Dick had a rather dry sense of humor, one that I find myself chuckling at even today.

As we patrolled together, we certainly experienced our share of memories to be included into the diaries. Such as the night we were patrolling through the town of Brooks in Dick's Maine State Police cruiser.

A young fellow from the neighboring town of Monroe, who recently had his driver's license revoked for a variety of reasons, sailed on by us heading in the opposite direction. Dick immediately turned around the cruiser and signaled for the young man to stop. Instead, we ended up in a short chase with the emergency lights flashing and the siren blaring right through the middle of downtown Brooks.

The chase quickly ended after the young fellow skidded into a nearby driveway, where he decided to bail out of the car, taking off on a dead run. Dick skidded to an abrupt halt, sprinting in hot pursuit directly behind the hefty little tyke. I quickly ran around the opposite side of the building, hoping to cut him off as he came my way.

The timing couldn't have been any better. I heard the pitter-patter of his stubby little legs heading in my direction. He was so intent on looking to see where Dick was, that he never noticed me hiding in the nearby shrubs. It was perfect timing, I upended him in the middle of the dirt driveway like a defensive tackle in the Super Bowl. We both were sprawled out on the ground like a couple of beached whales.

I could hear the loud beating of Dick's big feet rapidly coming toward us. He piled on the top of us, creating a big "pig-pile" of sorts, right in the middle of the dirt driveway.

Cars were stopping along the nearby road to witness the fiasco. A small crowd of onlookers gathered along the street. Surely they must have been highly impressed with the great show of justice they'd just witnessed

Quickly hoisting the chubby little outlaw back onto his feet, we dragged him over to the nearby cruiser and tossed him into the back seat with the handcuffs secured around his scrawny wrists. He never said a word. Instead, he appeared to be quite humbled by the entire affair.

Once inside the cruiser, Dick gathered the suspect's identification and was in the process of re-checking his license status. Suddenly, Dick glanced over my way. His face was all screwed up in a ball, obviously indicating some form of displeasure.

"Did you by any chance step in some dog shit, John?"

I was just about to ask him the same thing, as there was a definite smell of feces inside the closed and hot quarters of the police cruiser. Before I could respond, a meek little voice from the backseat muttered, "I think it's me! I've had an accident. I've shit myself!"

The raunchy smell was getting some putrid inside of the cruiser. I started gagging while floundering around searching for the door release, busting my way outside for a breath of fresh air. Actually, the raw feces smell was a bit more horrid than what the two of us could stand. Dick quickly exited the cruiser, coughing and gagging, on his side. Opening the back door of his vehicle, Dick ordered the detainee to get out.

Rather disgustedly, Dick advised him he could wait outside for the legal paperwork and the summons he planned on issuing.

Prior to this moment, our little buddy had been about to get a free ride to the crowbar hotel, but now there seemed to be a sudden change in plans. In this particular matter, Dick chose to "UN-arrest" our little prisoner and issue him a summons instead, with strict orders not to drive. Whether such an action was totally legal in law enforcement protocol, at that point it really didn't matter. This unusual case stunk. As such, it called for a little "curbside justice" resulting in the little bandit being released along the main street to wallow in his own mess. No pun intended!

However, one of the more classic memories I shared with Dick occurred late one summer evening in the town of Jackson.

Dick had an arrest warrant for an individual named Frank. Frank had been involved in several area burglaries after he had been on a wide crime spree for the past several weeks. It wasn't Frank's first encounter with the law. He had an extensive criminal history and he was known to run from the police. He also was noted to resort to violence in his efforts to escape, if the need be. Dick asked me to assist him in sneaking out behind the pop-up camper where Frank was living. The little camper was located a fair distance off the main road and well into the woods in the town of Jackson. The plan was for me to quietly sneak in behind the back side of the camper. Once I was in place, Dick would approach from the front, making his presence known.

It was pitch black and fairly late at night as we quietly maneuvered into position. We didn't know if Frank was inside, but it was time to find out. I positioned myself on the back side of the camper, ready for whatever happened. I got there without using my flashlight. I simply loved sneaking around in the so-called stealth mode.

Dick yelled, "Frank, this is the state police. You need to come out of the camper with your hands in the air. I have an arrest warrant for you!"

I could hear all kinds of commotion coming from inside the camper. Suddenly, out through the backside of the canvas-topped camper, plastic window and all, came Frank on the fly.

He sailed out through the air as if he'd been shot from a cannon. Landing squarely on his feet, he squirreled down through the woods like a whitetail deer in flight for its life.

We yelled for him to stop, all to no avail. Dick had the beam of his flashlight aimed squarely on the back of Frank's head, as we charged down through the woods on the narrow little foot path with both of us hot on his trail. He was zig-zagging back and forth, as he shot through the bushes like a rabbit being chased by a hound. Dick kept that beam of light on his head as we remained a short distance behind him.

Utilizing an old nighttime, foot-chasing technique, whenever we wardens were in hot pursuit of a fleeing subject through the woods in the dark of night, we simply turned off the flashlight, eliminating the source of light that the runner is depending upon to see where he's going. It worked miracles, and it worked once again.

Both Dick and I turned our lights off at the same time. A short distance in front of us we heard a loud crash, followed by another bang, and then a splash. Frank had run smack into several bushes and a dead tree or two, before falling belly first into a mud hole. The jig was up. He was quickly subdued and cuffed for the trip back out to the cruiser.

We were almost back at the campsite when Dick whispered, "John, I've got a problem. I've lost my damn service revolver somewhere down there in the woods."

I chuckled and said, "Don't feel bad, I've lost my portable radio somewhere down there, too!"

Frank didn't have a clue that we were missing any equipment, as he staggered along the trail in front of us.

Dick said, "We'd better go back looking for them now, or we'll never be able to retrace our tracks."

"What'll we do with Frank?" I inquired.

"I'll make sure he doesn't go anywhere," Dick snickered, as he unlocked the handcuffs securing Frank's wrists. Walking him over to a pine tree near the camper, Dick wrapped his arms around the base of the tree and reattached the cuffs firmly around his wrists. There was one thing for sure, Frank wasn't about to go anywhere unless he took that large pine with him.

"Frank's now connected to the pine tree hitching post," Dick smirked.

"What the hell are you guys doing?" Frank anxiously sputtered. "Hey, you can't just leave me here like this!" he yelled, as we slowly walked away.

"Hopefully, we'll be back in a minute, Frank. We're going looking for something," Dick assured him, as we shot back into the woods, retracing our steps, searching for the missing .357 hand gun and a portable radio.

Frank was yelling, "Hey! Hey! Where to hell are you guys going?" as we walked away.

After a few minutes of searching and retracing our footsteps, fortunately we located the missing items not far from where the apprehension was made. Frank's irritating voice could be heard echoing throughout the woods, as we slowly walked back his way. He sounded like a wounded coyote trying to rally its mates.

Frank seemed to be much happier to see us the second time around. All is well that ends well, the old saying goes. In this case, it ended well.

A crime once again was solved and justice was served. To my knowledge the old pine tree hitching post was never used again!

Poison in the Neighborhood

Not every story is one of humor, nor does it contain a little personal forgiveness for some errant human nature mistake that may have been committed by some poor soul who, in the heat of the moment, made a terrible mistake. There were some stories incorporated within the diaries that were downright disgusting as to how cruel and inconsiderate human nature at times can be. This story is one of them!

On April 22, 1979, I responded to a very emotional call from a distraught lady in the town of Troy.

Her dog, a young Doberman pup, had just dropped dead in her daughter's lap. She believed the sudden death of the puppy was due to a neighbor feeding the young animal a dose of some type of poison.

I quickly headed to this complaint after learning of two other dogs in the same neighborhood a few days earlier that had died rather mysteriously.

The visibly upset lady tried explaining through her sobs of sorrow, as to how her daughter and the young Doberman pup were playing together out on their front lawn. A strange man, who only recently had moved into the neighborhood with an elderly couple next door, called the young dog over to the garage next door, where he was observed feeding the little pup a handful of raw meat. Within minutes, the dog went into convulsions, dying in the lap of its young master.

Upon my arrival, I observed the dead dog stretched out on the lawn. It was stiff and rigid, appearing as if prior to its death that every muscle had tightened in its body.

The young girl and her mother were crying uncontrollably as they sadly related the facts of this senseless tragedy. They felt completely helpless in an effort to save the little pup.

In explicit detail, the youngster described seeing her new neighbor stepping outside. She noticed he appeared to be staring at the dog as he made what she took to be some sort of a snide comment that she couldn't hear. He proceeded to call the dog into the garage where he was hanging out. The pup obediently followed him inside. She watched as he removed a small package hidden from inside the wall of the garage. He mixed the contents of some type of powder into a handful of raw meat. Once he finished, he gave the raw meat to the little pup that by then was sitting by his feet, intently watching his every move. After the dog ate the meat, they both walked out of the garage.

"Suddenly the man began screaming and hollering at my dog, chasing it back over onto our property," the distraught teenager sobbed.

He disgustedly yelled, "You need to keep that *#!- damn dog of yours on your own land!" as he slowly turned away and walked back into the house.

The petrified little pup immediately ran up to her side, shaking and shivering with fear. Within a matter of minutes it began experiencing seizures. By the time her mother was made aware of what was happening, the dog was dead.

I took possession of the carcass and made arrangements for an autopsy on the dog to be conducted the next day by a local veterinarian.

As I was conducting my interviews and taking notes, I noticed the young man next door seemed to be intently watching my every move. Before I departed the area, he and his female friend loaded several personal belongings into their car and quickly left. I jotted down the vehicle's registration for future reference should I need it.

The results of the dog's autopsy the next morning confirmed the fact that the young pup had died from a massive dose of strychnine poisoning.

Returning to the scene, I confronted the old man living next door to the complainant, inquiring about the identity of the young man who had been staying with him for the past few days.

"Oh, that's my granddaughter and her new boyfriend, John!" he stated. "Why do you ask?"

Before I could respond, he sputtered, "John did something terribly wrong, didn't he? Last night he suddenly came running inside the house, telling her to grab her stuff, they were moving back to Augusta! He seemed to be in quite a hurry and he sure was acting real nervous," the old man related. "He did something really, really bad, didn't he?"

I described the morbid details involving the young girl and the death of her Doberman pup from the previous evening. Before I could finish telling the story, the old man's eyes filled with tears that were streaming down his cheeks like a little river.

He said, "My old dog! One that I've had for 16 years suddenly died the other day. He died shortly after they moved in with us. You don't suppose he killed my dog too, do you?" the old fellow sobbed.

I think he obviously knew the answer and what more could I say? "It appears as though he very well could have." I stated.

"John was some house guest to have around, huh?" I sarcastically remarked.

Unfortunately, the old man had already disposed of his pet, and I was unable to retrieve it to determine a cause of death.

I asked for permission to search his garage, seeking the bag of powder that the young girl had so explicitly described.

"Search any damn place you want," he disgustedly sputtered.

It wasn't long before I found a plastic bag containing a small amount of powdery substance stuffed in the wall, exactly where the young girl claimed it would be. In the nearby garbage can were the remains of a package of hamburger meat. I seized both articles for evidence and a chemical examination. The powder was confirmed to be strychnine, a deadly form of poison.

Based upon the information I'd obtained, I quickly applied for an arrest warrant for John before he could move elsewhere and continue to create havoc. According to the old man, John was working at a steel mill and living in the Augusta area.

Meanwhile, I had contacted Trooper Dick Reitchel and explained the situation to him. As it turned out, Dick was seeking John for the criminal thefts of two motorbikes within the same neighborhood. Dick had connected John to the thefts upon learning that he was attempting to sell the stolen motorbikes through *Uncle Henry's*, a popular swap and sell magazine that circulated throughout the Central Maine area.

Working together, as we so often did, I jumped into Dick's cruiser. By now we were determined to remove John from the streets just as soon as possible. Armed with the two arrest warrants, we headed for the steel mill in Augusta where John supposedly worked the second shift.

Upon entering the mill, as a matter of protocol, the shift foreman asked to see the warrants prior to putting us in contact with John. He then requested a crew member from the floor of the busy steel mill to bring John up to his office, so as not to cause a disturbance among the employees. Within minutes, John nonchalantly stepped into the office, unaware of what was going on.

Upon seeing Dick and me standing there in uniform, he suddenly bolted out through the door, fleeing down the hallway with both of us close on his heels. As he jumped onto the iron stairs leading back to the ground floor where the employees were attending to their tasks in the busy mill, we both tackled him. Together, we fell into a pile of flailing arms and legs at the bottom of the stairway, where my trooper buddy quickly grabbed him by the nape of the neck, hoisting him onto his feet and pinning him up against the wall.

The mill employees halted their work assignments and were loudly cheering and screaming at the spectacle unfolding before them, obviously pleased for a little abnormal entertainment to break up the boredom of the night shift. The only problem was, I couldn't distinguish just who it was they were cheering for. Somehow, I got the impression it wasn't for us!

I confiscated a set of sharply-filed brass knuckles with razor-like edges from John's pants pocket. He was ready to defend himself if the need arose. I was some thankful Dick and I had gone to the mill as a team. One on one, it might have been a little more treacherous for an officer to have made that arrest as easy as we did. John continued being quite a handful as he fought and resisted us all the way out to the police cruiser. As we dragged him along, kicking and fighting, the shift foreman advised John that his only purpose for ever returning to their facility would be to pick up his final paycheck. His employment at the mill was officially terminated at this time!

Justice sometimes works in a rather mysterious way. This case would certainly be one of those times.

At John's arraignment a few days later, he had several criminal charges against him. Surprisingly, John pleaded guilty to all of them, throwing himself upon the mercy of the court. In my case, he was assessed a simple fine of $50 and ordered to pay restitution of $35 to the little girl for her tragic loss. Due to the vicious circumstances of this incident, such a light penalty was a real slap in the face and an injustice in itself. In addition, John was ordered to serve 10 days in jail, all of it suspended, and he was placed on six months of probation, with the stipulation that he seek psychiatric counseling. Something he desperately needed I'd say!

There was no follow-up ordered by the court to see if in fact he ever did seek that counseling. The only portion of this legal sentence that I totally agreed with was the order for psychiatric help. In my view, John was in desperate need of treatment, and a lot of it! In this case, justice had definitely slipped through the cracks—big time! Any individual running around the countryside poisoning animals at random was capable of committing crimes far more serious. Today, it might be dogs, tomorrow it might be a person, maybe some poor individual whom John had taken a serious disliking to.

John should have been under intense monitoring by someone of authority, but instead he was allowed to slide back into society, free to come and go, almost as if nothing serious had ever happened. Even to this day, I expect there's a young lady out there somewhere who still experiences bad memories of that little puppy taking its final breaths as it lay in her lap.

It certainly appears that sometimes justice isn't meted out fairly. Was this one of those times? You decide!

A Passenger with God at the Helm

A few days after I was called to rescue wardens Tibbetts and Pidgeon from Carlton Bog in Troy when they literally were caught "up the creek without a paddle," I performed two more water rescues, only the next two were not quite as humorous as the first.

I received a phone call early on the morning of Oct. 16, 1981, from a member of the Unity Fire Department inquiring if I planned on coming to the search on Unity Pond. Their agency was ready to mount another search and they could use my assistance.

"What search?" I blankly asked, completely unaware of anything going on in the area. I'd just had a couple of days off and wasn't aware of any ongoing searches in my area.

"You didn't know?" he asked, sounding rather surprised. "We have a missing sailboater out on Unity Pond. The call came in late last night and you were on a day off. Another warden came to assist us, but he left after only a couple of hours. He said you'd be coming on duty in the morning and that you'd make contact with us, as he felt we'd done all we could for the night. I just assumed he had called you," the young fireman disgustedly sputtered.

"This is the first I've heard about it, but I'll be right over just as soon as I get dressed," I said.

I couldn't believe someone hadn't called the previous night, alerting me of the situation. There was an obvious miscommunication somewhere along the line.

The day before had started out as a warm Indian summer day. The temperatures were far above normal for that time of year. The Rev. Richard Woehr of Unity decided it would be a great afternoon for a season-ending sail out on Unity Pond before stowing away his small sailboat for the winter. As so often happens in cases such as this, he failed to notify anyone of his intentions before venturing out onto the lake at around 4 p.m. It was warm and a light wind provided ideal conditions for a relaxing afternoon out on the lake. Little did he realize it at the time, but it nearly became his last sail ever.

Richard's wife returned home later that evening. She knew her husband had planned to attend a church meeting elsewhere, so when he wasn't home she wasn't overly concerned. She simply assumed he was at his meeting doing God's work. It wasn't until 11:30 p.m. when he still wasn't home that she truly began to worry. She then noticed that their small sailboat was missing from their front porch. She quickly hurried down to the pond, where she found his car parked in the normal spot where he left it when he went sailing. Only then did she realize he was in danger—grave danger. Panic set in as she alerted the authorities of her situation.

We later learned from the Rev. Woehr that during the afternoon as he was enjoying his time on the water, the wind suddenly switched directions and the temperatures rapidly plummeted. The rapid change in weather is quite typical of fall in New England. A cold front had worked its way into our region, bringing along with it high winds and much colder temperatures.

The reverend started back across the lake, tacking into the wind hoping to reach his destination in the stiff breeze. Simultaneously the temperature plunged. The sudden change in wind direction carried him farther and farther away from his intended destination. The reverend realized he wasn't going to reach his vehicle, when a large gust of wind hit the small craft, turning it over and dumping him into the cool water. The Rev. Woehr desperately searched for his life jacket inside the submerged boat, but couldn't find it.

By then, it was well after 5 p.m. The sun was setting and the wind continued to howl a gale. The waves were splashing around him, with white caps encompassing the water for as far as he could see. In October, very few people occupy the camps along the shoreline, so his calls for help went unanswered.

Grabbing hold of the boat's flotation pad, placing it firmly beneath him, he attempted to swim back toward shore quite some distance away. But the high wind and rough waves battled his every stroke. He realized he'd never make it under the existing conditions. Returning back to the overturned boat as a last resort, he barely managed to climb up on top of the capsized craft. Numbness settled in his arms and legs and a tremendous fear was beginning to overtake the pastor.

The Rev. Woehr said his faith in God simultaneously provided him with a sudden burst of inner strength and a sense of calmness. He felt as though he'd temporarily been saved from his own demise.

He considered diving underneath the boat to retrieve a paddle, but he knew if he tried he wouldn't have any strength left to climb back upon the overturned boat. By now, mentally drained and physically strapped, he sat astride the small half-submerged sailboat for the rest of the night.

A search was initiated in the wee morning darkness, but the searchers remained far away from where the sailboat had floated during the night. The small boat was upside down and bobbing along in the windswept waves, far away from where they had started.

The distraught minister was unable to draw attention to his plight. He realized he was at the mercy of the Almighty and needed a whole lot of luck.

For the searchers, it was difficult to know where to start. After all, the pond was more than six miles long and quite wide. There was a very slim chance of ever finding the missing man in the black of night, as he bobbed up and down in the waves and fought a constant howling wind. It was hoped that at daylight, searchers would have a better chance locating the reverend. But many of the rescuers feared the worst.

They were simply looking for the sailboat, and then trying to figure out where the reverend may have drowned to start the recovery of a body.

In the meantime, the minister stated, "I was tempted to end the bitter cold and suffering myself by just slipping over the side of the boat and giving up," the Rev. Woehr recalled. "A thousand things went through my mind. Being a preacher, I did a lot of praying, not so much in desperation, but just plain talking to God. I kept telling myself to hang on just a little while longer," he said. "I was desperately trying to stay alive."

Upon my arrival at Unity Pond that next morning, the searchers had just spotted the sailboat at the far end of the lake. Several of them were heading that way by boat. I quickly shot around the pond in my vehicle so it could provide heat on land if the reverend was still alive.

When the searchers finally arrived at the overturned sailboat, the Rev. Woehr was still clinging to it, barely able to speak, and completely unable to move his legs. An ambulance met us on a nearby camp road at the far end of the lake. We carried the reverend to a waiting stretcher for some much-needed medical attention. His body temperature was a mere six degrees higher than what hospital staffers considered to be fatal. Immediately, warm saline solution and heated oxygen was administered to him, and he was whisked away to the hospital where he remained for a few days—extremely fortunate to be alive.

In this particular case, I honestly believe there was another unseen passenger on that overturned sailboat, God himself, sparing the reverend from what could have been a tragedy.

Mr. Woehr fortunately lived to tell about his terrifying ordeal, unlike the person involved in a water rescue situation I was called to the very next evening.

Three water rescues in a week, one humorous, one extremely fortunate, and the other not fortunate. Yet more memories for the diaries—I never knew what catastrophe or incident would be coming next.

The life of a warden had its share of surprises and catastrophies lurking on the horizon. I guess that's what I liked about the profession—never knowing from one minute to the next what incident might be right around the corner.

Another Act of Mental Cruelty

Late in the evening of Oct. 17, 1981, Deputy Warden Scott Sienkiewicz, Norman Gilbert and I were called to a search for a 23-year-old man who'd left his home in Burnham early in the afternoon to do a little duck hunting along the river near his house.

According to the family, he was dressed in warm clothes and wearing chest waders. The young Burnham man was very healthy and woods-wise, according to his family. Late that evening, after he failed to return home, family and friends organized a small search party of their own, obviously not wanting to involve the authorities. A few members of that crew had obviously been drinking and, as such, they chose to handle the matter by themselves.

It wasn't until much later in the evening when Warden Gilbert, Deputy Warden Sienkiewicz and I were the first authorities to arrive on the scene. Some of the members of the private search party quickly voiced their opinions about where we should go and what should be done next. At that point in time, the search was in a state of total unorganized chaos, to put it mildly.

Upon our arrival, we immediately put out a request to the area fire department to assist us with manpower. As usual, a number of local volunteer firemen rallied to provide their expertise and total cooperation in conducting an organized search. They were teams of men who were organized and experienced searchers and were willing to be sent to specific spots along the river, searching for the missing duck hunter in an organized way. They knew where and how to search, much to the disgruntlement of those few boisterous drinkers who were watching from afar and were a bit vocal about having any of the authorities around.

It was obvious there were some within their group who appeared to despise game wardens or any other forms of authority. They made no bones about wishing we were not there, and how they'd rather be handling the matters themselves. Their blatant arrogance was the obvious result of plenty of liquor. After their own failed attempts to locate the missing young man, the distraught family members decided to notify the authorities.

Later in the evening the volunteer searchers from the fire department, most of them who knew the area extremely well, reported back to the command post that nothing had been found. The effort had proven futile. But the search continued, well into the nighttime hours, despite the hindrance of those who wished it hadn't.

Suddenly, word was sent back up river from one of the inebriated searchers who had gone off on his own. He claimed to have found the missing young man. According to the unsubstantiated messages being relayed back through the thick woods to the command center, the missing hunter had a broken leg and needed to be transported up along the stream and out to the main road.

Several crews were quickly dispatched downstream to accommodate the victim's needs. Immediately, I requested the Clinton ambulance to be dispatched to the area. A medically equipped crew was assembled to assist the men in carrying the victim back out of the woods. The family members, including the young man's wife, were notified that their loved one was found as they hurried to the command post hoping for the best news possible.

Sadly, I was forced to tell them the good news was nothing more than a sick rumor started by a couple of drunks seeking a little personal attention. They had been drinking and didn't care for the way things were being conducted.

We never found out who played the evil prank, and probably it was a good thing we didn't. Without a doubt, any form of professionalism we were trying to maintain that cold, fall night had quickly gone out the window. I wouldn't have been surprised to have witnessed a public lynching by those people who had gathered trying to locate these sick pranksters. Something told me there would have been a little poetic justice in the wind, had anyone found them—tempers were hot, and the mood was ripe for an all-out brawl.

By then, it was quite obvious that any additional attempts to locate the young man during the middle of the night would be fruitless and futile. Any sense of organization had completely disappeared, thanks to those who chose to derail the effort. As such, the search effort was suspended until daybreak. I could only hope by then that cooler heads and minds would prevail, and we'd be able to see where we were going with the search.

I barely slept that night, still irate over the inconsiderate drunks who played such a horrible hoax upon the missing man's family members who were suffering badly enough as it was. But to have their hopes lifted and to be totally relieved to hear their loved one was still alive, only to have the rug pulled out from beneath them a few minutes later was inexcusable! It truly can be a sick world we live in at times, and this was one of those times.

The next day, the body of young Tim Rice was discovered submerged in a deep pool of water a short distance downstream from his home. Apparently, he had shot a duck that fell into the deep pool of water flowing down the river. As Tim waded out into the river to retrieve his cache, the water filled his chest waders and dragged him down, making it impossible for him to swim. His lifeless body was transported to the main highway, where a somber crowd of family, friends, and searchers watched as the body was placed inside a hearse.

I hoped somewhere in that somber and silent crowd of onlookers were the drunken men who the night before had so stupidly created false hope and additional pain for an already distraught family, simply because they wanted to have a little fun and generate attention for themselves. I doubt they'd recognize their own sins, nor would they ever feel any guilt. Folks in that state of mind never do; their own undoings are always the fault of someone else.

Strangely, during that one week in October I'd responded to three water-related searches and rescues.

One was rather humorous, involving two of our own; one was extremely lucky, the good reverend had God on his side; and one was a real tragedy.

They all provided yet another cluster of memories for the diaries. I only wish they all were humorous, but unfortunately in this line of work, the good often comes with the bad, and sometimes the damn right ugly.

These series of memories included bits of all three.

Sometimes Justice Doesn't Make Any Sense

I had inherited a high-powered scope from an old friend who thought the item might come in handy for my law enforcement occupation. Anxious to have a new toy, I decided to check out its capabilities as I headed out onto a remote camp road in Unity.

It was an exceptionally warm late summer day as I slowly drove along the narrow dead-end camp road, searching for any signs of activity around the lake where I could try out my new scope. It was a time of the year when most of the campers around the lake had already headed home for the winter. With fall quickly approaching, many of them returned to their camps on weekends only, if at all. So, I wasn't too concerned about disturbing anyone staying in the few camps along this narrow road. I simply assumed I was all alone out along the side of the lake. My intent was to observe any fishermen, or any other activity that might be occurring near the popular gathering spot on the lake, known as the "railroad trestle."

The Belfast and Moosehead Lake train crosses the trestle on the western side of the pond. The metal bridge over the outlet from Unity pond allows the slow-moving train to run from Burnham to Belfast and back. Most of the time, the cargo being hauled by the train consisted of grain being delivered to local farmers or loads of wood being hauled off to market.

The railroad trestle was a favorite hangout for scores of swimmers and fishermen. Its location was a place where most folks felt they too were all alone and off in their own little private setting. On this particular day, I noticed five young people, four males and a female, walking down the railroad tracks heading for the railroad bridge. They were wearing their swimming suits and carrying a large paper bag, which I assumed contained either soda or beer.

I stopped in the middle of the camp road in a spot where I could plainly observe their activities with my new bionic eye. Quickly assembling the scope onto its tripod, I carefully placed the contraption upon the hood of my cruiser. I began observing these folks to make sure they weren't law breakers and, moreso, to test out my new bionic eye! It worked perfectly, far better than anything I ever expected. I was able to zero in on the group close enough to identify what brand of cigarettes they were smoking. I watched as they removed a six-pack of Old Milwaukee beer from the paper bag.

Lordy, lordy, the next thing I knew, they'd removed their bathing suits and were skinny-dipping off of the train bridge. They were having a grand old time, laughing and joking, swimming, and drinking—a typical party with good friends.

I continued watching as they finally finished their beers, tossed the empty cans into the pond and watched them float downstream. They each threw at least one can, with the exception of one young man, who threw two cans into the water below them.

I wrote down as thorough a description of them as I could, so as to be able to identify them later on. My intent was to round them up after they readied themselves to head back to where I assumed their car was parked, and to issue them all court summonses for the littering of beer cans they'd thrown from the bridge. Except for the female, it was kind of hard describing them, other than by their hair color, their height, and roughly their weight.

I even managed to watch a little sexual hanky-panky between one of the males and the female, as they stood between the rails on the trestle.

I was flopping around on the hood trying to stay focused with my bionic eye, swinging the lens first one way and then the other. I suddenly heard a woman's voice coming from the camp right beside where I had stopped. The lady scared the bejesus out of me, to put it mildly. Up until then, I thought I was all alone.

"Quite a show isn't it John?" she chuckled.

Startled, and a little embarrassed to know that now I was being watched myself, I turned around to see this elderly lady, who shall remain nameless, standing in the doorway with her binoculars in her hand. She was watching the same show as I was.

"Oh, wouldn't it be nice to be young again," she seductively smiled.

I thought to myself, "Oh God, don't try to seduce me, Mrs. Robinson!" as she appeared to have a little twinkle in her aging eyes.

I replied, "Oh yeah, it certainly would. But did you see them throw that litter into the pond?" I was desperately trying to convince her I was only there to do my job. Which I kind of was!

"Oh, they do that all the time!" She shrugged my remarks off with a brief wave of her hands.

"Well, I'm going to teach them a little lesson in the environmental laws!" I responded. I wanted her to realize that I was making a case and not simply spying on a group of young skinny-dippers. Whether I thoroughly convinced her or not, I'll never know. Somehow, I don't believe I was too convincing of anything at that time!

"How are you going to get to them before they leave?" she asked "They came to the bridge from over in Burnham you know, and you certainly can't drive across the water from here," she snickered.

"I'm sure they've parked over on the camp road over by the railroad crossing on the other side of the lake," I stated. "When they get ready to leave, I figure I'll have just enough time to high-tail it down through town and over to that camp road. By the time they walk back to their vehicle, get loaded into the car and head out, I should be right there. I'm going to have to skedaddle though! They'll be coming out on the Prairie Road and I'll catch them before they leave!" I boldly stated.

Once the swimming and sex were over, these young-uns dried themselves off, put their swimsuits back on, and slowly started hiking back up the tracks from whence they had come. It was time for me to pack up and roll.

Driving like a bat out of Haiti, I caught up with them just as they were coming to the end of the camp road in Burnham.

Blocking the roadway, I sauntered up to the car, identifying myself as the local game warden. Politely I explained that I was going to issue them all a summons for the littering violations.

"How to hell do you know we littered?" one of the males quickly challenged.

I bluntly stated, "Look! I've been watching you from over across the pond! You were drinking 16-ounce cans of Old Milwaukee beer. You weren't wearing your bathing suits," and then pointing to the apparent self-appointed mouthpiece for the group, I said, "and you sir, you threw two cans into the water while the rest of your buddies threw only one!"

Then quickly directing my attention to the guy and the girl seated next to each other, I said, "And you two," as I was looking directly at them, "well, you two know what you did out there!"

I didn't have to say anymore. I could see the stunned and shocked looks on their faces.

The driver humbly stated to his passengers, "Hey guys, the man knows what he is talking about, we're guilty and we know it! Can we have some time officer, to take care of this in court?" he pathetically begged.

I replied, "No problem," as I gathered information from each of them in order to write the summonses out for their Belfast District Court appearance.

They were being very cooperative, so I generously gave them a few weeks to come up with the needed funds to pay a fine.

On court day, four of the five appeared before Judge Ed Smith, entering their guilty pleas for the crime of littering. The fifth gentleman, who just happened to have been the one who threw the two cans, had called the court asking for an extension of time due to an emergency he was experiencing back home. He was told to report to court the following week at the same time.

Judge Smith asked for my report on the incident.

I said, "Yes, Your Honor, I witnessed these people throwing beer cans off from the railroad trestle and into Unity Pond while they were there for an afternoon swim. They each threw one can apiece—there was nothing more than that, Your Honor!"

I didn't bother to describe the entire events as they really unfolded. That would have been just a little bit more than what the Judge needed to know!

After a brief lecture from Smitty on the ills of littering, he assessed each of them a $50 fine. He accepted their guilty pleas and quickly motioned them out of the court room, ordering them to go to the clerk's office and pay their fines.

The following week, the young man who had thrown the two cans into the water made his own appearance before Smitty, pleading guilty to the charges leveled against him.

Smitty, once again asked for the details.

I simply said, "Yes, Your Honor. This man accompanied the four people who were here last week for the same offense. The only difference being, Your Honor, that this gentleman threw two cans into the water, instead of one!"

I thought surely the judge would remember the littering cases from the previous week.

With yet another stern lecture regarding the horrors of littering, Smitty told the young man, "I find you guilty of the charge of littering. That will be a $25 fine. Go with the officer and take care of it outside."

I was quite befuddled by the vast difference in fines between him and his four companions who the week before had paid $50 each for their sins. This young man had thrown twice as many cans and yet his fine was half as much as theirs!

As we slowly walked down the corridor to the clerk's office in order for him to pay his fine, I disgustedly stated, "I'm some damn glad you didn't throw a six-pack of cans into the lake! At the financial rate this judge is assessing fines today, I'd have to have paid you $75 to come here!"

We both left the courthouse laughing over the noticeable differences in fines. My new friend was extremely happy to have waited a week before making his one and only court appearance. I couldn't say as though I blamed him! I just wondered what his buddies must have thought when he returned home to tell his story.

Oh well, justice sometimes works in a mysterious way. This was one of them!

Another Trooper to Break In

It was in the early month of July 1982, when yet another Maine state trooper moved into the Unity area. During my 12 years of patrolling the area as the district game warden, I'd witnessed several troopers come and go for various reasons. Some decided law enforcement wasn't really their forte while others had proven themselves within the agency and moved up the ladder of success and on to bigger and better positions.

Trooper Reitchel was the latest to be promoted when he accepted a criminal detective's position within his department. His promotion was a well-deserved one. I knew he'd serve the agency well. No longer would we be cruising the same roads, chasing the bad guys and sharing great memories together.

It seemed as though I'd just get comfortable working with one of these troopers and like a magical wave of the hand, suddenly they were gone.

Trooper Mark Nickerson became the next member of the Maine State Police to invade my sacred territory when he laterally transferred from the Greenville patrol to Unity. Mark joined the state police in 1977, following along in his dad's footsteps. Mark's recently retired father, Capt. Millard Nickerson, was a highly-skilled criminal investigator within the Detective's Division of the Maine State Police. He actually had been instrumental in founding the department's investigative division. Captain Nick, as he was called, had a rather colorful and interesting career, investigating more than one case that brought him national recognition for his efforts.

Unfortunately, I and a couple of other wardens who were just starting our young careers were dragged out of class at warden school one day by the large burly investigator to undergo a criminal interrogation against ourselves. This official investigator's stern looks and intimidating demeanor would scare the confession out of the hardest of criminals.

That particular in-house investigation was a story in itself. One where I didn't know but my dream career was about to come to a sudden and abrupt ending, simply because of an innocent purchase of some stolen material we had bought from a fellow officer in our warden class. A man who apparently had some rather sticky fingers back in his day of previous employment, and prior to his being hired by the department as a new warden recruit.

Innocently, I'd purchased a new, still-in-the-package stereo system for my cruiser. The price was one I couldn't pass up after my brother warden explained how he had received two of the same items as Christmas presents and he simply wanted to get rid of the extra. Another classmate purchased a new pair of snowshoes for a price he too couldn't pass up. These shoes, according to our classmate, were apparently extras he was given from a sporting company he used to work for.

The stories sounded reasonable and credible, and the items were bought in good faith. After all, he was one of us, an official officer of the law, who swore to protect, obey, and honor all of the laws of Maine and the country. In accepting that oath, he was expected to carry himself in a manner that exemplified law enforcement and not discredit it!

Long story short, our fellow classmate was arrested and criminally charged for theft one afternoon while a few of us were together, in uniform, shopping at a local Bangor shopping mall. He was detained by the store's security guards as we all were about to depart the store, and that was the last we ever saw of him. Meanwhile, those of us who had bought the items we had from him, did so in good faith.

We were not penalized in any way, other than receiving that eye-opening experience and the humility of being hoodwinked by one of our own. Then there was the dreaded fear of being let go from the great careers we'd worked so hard to get!

It was a great learning experience to say the least. Inside lessons on a real interrogation from a hard-nosed grilling by one of Maine's top cops! Captain Nick certainly left his mark on the state police. He had served the state well.

Then, several years later, I was pairing up with his son. Hopefully we too would be leaving our own legacies within the law enforcement profession—both of us doing a job that we both loved. Having yet another trooper to break in and to share experiences with was something to look forward to.

Little did I realize it at the time what a treat Mark's presence would become. Some of those experiences we shared still make me shudder to this very day. I don't say that in a negative way by any means. I base my comments on what a wild and independent member of the state police I'd be sharing the rest of my law enforcement career with.

We both had a stubborn and independent streak with our bosses, and were quick to resist any new out-of-the-norm changes made by management. Especially if those changes took away our own freedoms in the manner in which we performed the very jobs we were hired for.

Plus, we both loved the careers and, for the most part, we loved the people we served. To say we created a long list of memories for the diaries would be an understatement at best. Hell, I could write an entire book on just the scrapes and episodes we both got into.

First of all, jumping into Mark's police cruiser was like climbing into a capsule on some Disney thriller ride. I swear, Mark cruised at one speed and one speed only. That was flat-arse-out. It was a real challenge riding along as a passenger in his cruiser, especially when a crisis arose that required an immediate response. There were times when I felt as though I was a front seat passenger in a low flying jet at Mach 2 or more, as we soared across the highways en route to a variety of dire situations.

I jokingly tell folks that it was nearly a year after I'd retired before my eyeballs finally caught up with my head, especially after flying over back roads at G-forces that normal people never got to experience.

Through it all, I never once felt that Mark didn't have the rocket under his complete control. Mark's expertise behind the wheel gained him a position at the Maine State Police Academy teaching pursuit driving. For several years he taught more than one young trooper how to safely steer a ship on dry land at ultra-high speeds. Mark was an expert at what he did, there was no doubt about it.

I simply reckoned that practice made perfect, and there was one thing about it, Mark was always practicing. There were a few times when my shorts could properly avouch for the fact I'd been to the edge of life and back. Yup, unlike the others who had preceded Mark as Maine state troopers within my patrol area, this fast trip down memory lane was going to be one hell of a show. Every day would be a new experience.

One of Mark's best attributes was his uncanny ability to recognize a drunk driver. He could pick out an intoxicated operator in a field of more than 100 vehicles in a demolition derby for cripes sake.

He had an eagle eye for noticing the obvious in spotting these folks. In all probability, his uncanny ability to recognize the threat on our highways saved several lives over the years as he removed these threatening menaces from the highways. At the last count, I believe Mark had nabbed more than 1,000 drunk drivers, holding them accountable for their sins—a record that probably will stand for many years, if not forever, in the history of the Maine State Police.

Just prior to Mark's retirement, he was sent to Washington D.C., where he received a National State Police Officers Distinguished Award for his unending efforts to remove the drunken drivers from our highways. The award that was personally presented to him by President Bill Clinton. Quite an honor for a Maine trooper, picked from several of those from all across the country.

Mark and I worked extremely well together. We both ended our great careers patrolling the same area. And to think we did it without getting fired or even physically hurt in the process. Although, more than once, we received our little reprimands and had frequent ups and downs with the powers to be, especially after pushing matters to the edge on those issues that we felt strongly about.

Mark related to his boss that there must have been something vile in the Unity drinking water that brought out the stiff independence and stubbornness both he and I seemingly shared. I'm not so damn sure that he wasn't right—the water did taste funny and we always seemed to create our own personnel problems.

One thing we both did share was the fact that during our illustrious careers it was very evident that neither of us ever climbed up the managerial ladder of success. Looking back upon it today, I'm some damn glad I didn't.

The times were constantly changing, as were working habits and philosophies, and none of it was for the better. For many of us old-timers, not all of these changes were made with the best interests in mind of the public we served, or for those whom we dedicated our lives to!

The citizens of Maine often were the real losers in some of these command decisions.

Good Day to Shoot a Moose

In every patrol district across the state there seemingly were a few people who expressed a nasty and rather defiant attitude when they found themselves in the presence of their local game warden or police officer. At one time or another, every law enforcement officer experienced a similar reaction when they came face to face with those who were not supportive of their department's mission. Whether the meeting was in an official capacity, or simply a chance greeting along the street, it was obvious some folks who crossed our path weren't about to say anything complimentary to an officer of the law. More often than not, a little liquid spirit enhanced their abilities to challenge authority.

When I began my new career in the Waldo County area, especially in Burnham, some of the older residents treated my presence as if I were a carrier of the black plague invading their private territory. Mind you, not all of the folks were that way. Some of them were actually pleased to see a new face in a warden's uniform. But, for the most part, the old die-hard poachers looked at my uniform and badge as if I were the commander of the enemy camp, ready to attack them in a moment's notice.

It was obvious, I was definitely regarded by some of these people as a serious threat to their very existence, or should I say their nightly types of lifestyle. They were reluctant to share a cordial relationship, or even a simple greeting, with the likes of someone like me. To them, I was from the enemy camp. Those who did offer a friendly greeting or gesture made sure they expressed any act of kindness when no one from the general public was watching.

At the very start of my young career, night hunting was an accepted tradition within this area and by golly, no brand new, badge-toting, baby game warden was going to break that tradition. Not as far as they were concerned anyway.

It took a whole lot of patience and persuasion on my part before I ever was welcomed to wander in among them. But as the years passed, many of those old die-hard poachers I had been forced to deal with actually became some of the best folks I ever got to know. I had the distinct pleasure of running across one of these defiant, arrogant folks Aug. 9, 1982, as I exited my cruiser in front of the Unity hardware store.

I was minding my own business, not paying attention to anyone, when I heard a loud voice screaming at me from up the street a short distance away. I glanced up in time to see a notorious law-breaker named Moe staggering down the side of the road as he attempted to walk my way. It was quite obvious Moe was higher than a kite in a thundershower, either from the booze he was drinking or from the drugs he had inhaled. I knew him to indulge in both at every opportunity he could.

Moe was a big man. I'd estimate him to be a little over 6 feet tall and weigh a whopping 300 pounds or more. His shirt was unbuttoned and his hair was messed up.

It looked like he had stuck his finger in a light socket and the electrical shock had stood those few long strands of his dirty hair straight up. I swear he had drool flowing from his mouth as he started screeching at me.

I could barely make out what he was yelling, "Ugh – ugh – Today would be a good day to go shoot a moose wouldn't it, John? Huh huh." I bet if Moe screamed that foolish statement once, he shouted it a dozen times, over and over!

Nearly the entire street could hear his senseless bellowing as he staggered my way. It was obvious Moe was trying to tempt me into paying a little attention to him, but I didn't bite. I simply ignored the fool and continued on inside the hardware store to conduct my business.

Moe remained outside the store for a few minutes, screaming the same old song, over and over, "Yup, today would be a good day for me to go shoot a moose, John boy. Ugh ugh!"

His grunting and mumbling kind of reminded me of a big old pig, stuck hip deep in a slop bin. By the time I'd completed my business within the store and had talked to the few patrons inside doing business, Moe was long gone.

The previous day, my new trooper pal Mark Nickerson had been to Moe's residence searching for an escapee from the Thomaston State Prison. The rumor mill had it that Moe and his buddy Dennis were harboring the escaped fugitive, but neither Moe nor Dennis would let Mark conduct a search of their premises for the missing man without a warrant authorizing the search. At the time, Mark lacked the needed information and probable cause to obtain a search warrant authorizing him to enter the residence. But it was quite obvious from the way these nimrods were acting that the missing fugitive was nearby.

The very next day, after my little escapade with Moe in front of the hardware store, Mark requested my assistance. He inquired if I could meet him along Depot Street in Unity, almost in the same exact location where Moe had been screaming the day before. Mark had corralled a man that he believed was the missing fugitive from Thomaston State Prison.

He had him handcuffed in the backseat of his cruiser. Mark inquired if I would accompany him for the long ride to the Belfast jail just in case things took a sudden turn for the worse. The uncooperative male secured in the back of Mark's cruiser refused to give his name and would not provide any identification. His description matched that of the missing fugitive, but just like Moe the day before, this man was higher than a kite in a hurricane. Again, either on booze or drugs.

The only information he would volunteer was, "My name is Ray! Some call me Ray-Ray, some call me Gay Ray, but today I'm just plain Ray! You got it you *#$!!- holes?" the man screamed as he twisted and turned in the backseat where he was tethered. To put it bluntly, Ray was nothing more than an intoxicated wise guy. He wasn't about to cooperate with us in any way.

Long story short, Ray ended up being that escaped fugitive and he commented as to how he'd been safely hidden at the trailer park just outside of town by his two good buddies, Moe and Dennis. From all appearances it looked as though they'd been having one constant party, day after day, night after night, ever since his burst of freedom carried him far away from the state prison. Mark quickly obtained an arrest warrant for both Moe and Dennis, charging them with harboring a fugitive.

With Ray-Ray safely back behind bars at the Thomaston facility, the next day Mark and I set out to arrest Moe and Dennis—that is, if we could find them. We were hot on their trail in the Waterville/Winslow area. But every lead we followed up on, they were one step ahead of us, totally unaware that we were nearby with warrants for their arrest in our hands. It wasn't long before a Winslow police officer spotted their vehicle headed out of town, but he was unable to catch up to it.

He provided us with a direction of travel and a thorough description of the two male occupants. There was no doubt whatsoever that they were the ones we wanted. The rocket man placed the cruiser into overdrive and we were off and flying. With the blue lights flashing and the siren blaring, we shot across the roads like a speeding bullet headed for its target.

As I did so many times before whenever we were on a mission, I tightened my seat belt as tight as it would go, sucked my buns firmly into the passenger's seat, and made damn sure that I had a firm death grip on the dashboard. In other words, I once again was hanging on for dear life.

Moe and Dennis never stood a chance—we were behind them before they knew what hit them. When they finally pulled over to the side of the highway, they were ordered out of the vehicle.

The next thing I saw was a highly inebriated Moe sprawled out in the ditch, with his arms flopping wildly as he tried getting up but he couldn't. He looked like a beached whale, stuck high and dry on a sand dune. His arms continued flailing wildly, but he couldn't muster the strength to stand up. Like a few days before, he was higher than a kite!

I couldn't resist the temptation to stand over him and scream in the same tone he'd used on me earlier, "Ugh – ugh. Today's a good day to go to jail isn't it Moe? Huh – huh! Yup. A good day to go to jail! Ugh, ugh!"

I kept shouting that foolish statement over and over. I wanted to be sure he got the drift of my message, hoping that in turn he'd see just how arrogant his remarks had been the day before. But given the condition he was in, hell I don't think he had the slightest clue where he was, what was happening, or anything I was saying!

It was a great feeling on the long ride to the crowbar hotel, knowing that justice had once more prevailed, and the criminal element faced yet another minor setback.

It wouldn't be our last run-in with Moe and his team of cronies. They'd provide us with far more entertainment than most folks could comprehend. Over the years we found ourselves constantly dealing with the likes of them.

One thing for sure, my new trooper buddy Mark and I would have a whole host of memories to write about. A good many of those diary entries involved people just like Moe, Dennis, and Ray. Folks like them provided those of us in law enforcement with what we called "job security!" As long as they were around, our jobs were definitely secure!

Conclusion

The years passed by quickly. Along with that passage of time came many changes in our working habits, and the methods of performing the law enforcement duties. The job was no longer providing the enjoyment it once did. The changing times and the new politics associated with the profession were certainly not in favor of those of us who once thoroughly enjoyed our professions.

Shift work had been implemented and ridiculous and totally unmanageable mileage restrictions were a serious deterrent to maintaining our patrol techniques—techniques that had been so effective in the past.

I was finding myself being disciplined for doing the job I'd been hired for, for driving more miles than I was allotted, and for a whole host of other dictated work habits.

The mileage restriction alone brought about a brief period of time when I was forbidden to use my vehicle. If I needed to respond to a complaint, I was told to phone the boss. He'd take me to the complaint and bring me back home. There was certainly a loss of the great freedoms and utilization of our own judgment that we were once entrusted with to perform our duties, without the interference from our own agency. These new procedures basically were preventing us from doing our jobs.

The courts were no longer taking many of our cases serious and through it all, people within my district had lost that personal contact they once had with individual law enforcement officers in the area. The profession was no longer as enjoyable as it once had been.

I suddenly found myself working dictated hours that I hated, while being forbidden to work the ones I knew I should have been. I was working in areas where I didn't have a clue where I was going, covering for other wardens who were either off from their assigned shift, or on a day off, which left me dealing with people I didn't know. I suddenly felt like an overgrown baby sitter with no real future ahead.

We wardens were being chastised and penalized for driving too many miles, for working too many hours, and for failing to represent the public as the front office felt we should.

As a result, we were given poor efficiency ratings because our expected work was not as thorough as it once had been. The nit-picking from the top was unbearable. Prominent and powerful politicians in Augusta were publicly crucifying the wardens in the field. They did so by conducting public meetings where disgruntled folks who had received summonses from a warden enforcing the very laws these politicians had passed, were publicly allowed to voice their unsavory opinions and comments against those wardens doing their jobs.

In other words, these political hacks were publicly crucifying the wardens' conduct for performing their official duties, in order to make themselves look good to the public and gather a vote in the process. Yet, it was the politicians who had passed the laws we wardens were enforcing!

It was discouraging to see folks who were awaiting their time before a judge so boisterously speaking out at these hearings. They had yet to have their cases adjudicated by the courts, as they should have been.

And those who were in higher management positions within the agency remained completely silent, not wanting to challenge the politicians controlling the department's purse strings. Instead, they simply allowed their own employees to get a public crucifying rather than doing what was right.

I saw the writing on the wall—I felt the brunt of punishment for doing the job I once loved, and I knew, just like those wardens before me, that my time had come and it was my time to go.

Conclusion

I needed to leave! I needed to leave while I still could, and before that stubborn resistance to these new changes and my big mouth got me into a position where I might be fired.

I now realize exactly how those wardens preceding me had felt when they too made the move. Those pioneers that we all admired from our earlier days, also had said, "We've seen the best of it!" and they moved into that new era of life beyond being a game warden.

I wanted to leave without an attitude of pure bitterness and with a collection of great memories in hand. The times were definitely changing and, simply put, I wasn't ready for any of it!

So it was, in June of 1990, I pulled the plug and left my gear at the Augusta storehouse as many of my fellow wardens had done before me. I emotionally signed off from the radio for one last time, with no regrets for the great career I'd had. It was a sad and emotionally trying time, as I knew the great life I'd lived would be no more.

But looking ahead, I decided to make a political run for high sheriff in Waldo County. Rather miraculously, I was elected! I even had the honor of receiving a letter from one of my most notorious old-time poaching buddies within the region, along with a check for $200 to use toward my public campaign for the high office.

The enclosed note stated:

"John, please use this money to go toward your sheriff's campaign. We all hope you get elected because then we'll know just where to hell you are for a change!"

That simple note from an old adversary warmed my heart as I quickly cashed the check to see if it was for real, and it was! Humorously, even my old sparring partner Grover contributed to my campaign. He gave me a dime!

With a new law enforcement career as sheriff, there would be more real stories for a new version of life's amazing cop tales! My old career and that long-ago dream had come to a final end, and a new dream was about to begin.

God had given me a great ride over the years and life was definitely good! Here's hoping you enjoyed some of that journey that I've shared with you as much as I have enjoyed living it.

Maine's sporting public was the best, and the folks I dealt with on both sides of the aisle, in my mind, are still my friends to this very day!

About the Author

John grew up in the small York County town of Shapleigh, Maine, where his entire family was heavily involved in various forms of the law enforcement profession. In September of 1970, a childhood dream became a reality when John became the newest member of the Maine Warden Service, a position he held until his retirement in 1990. Upon his retirement, John ran for political office and was elected Waldo County Sheriff, replacing his good friend, Sheriff Stanley Knox. John remained the county sheriff for two terms, serving the county from 1991-1999.

John's writing career came about thanks to *Republican Journal* editor Beth Staples, who convinced him to do a bi-weekly column of actual events and stories recorded in the young lawman's daily diaries. Keeping a diary was something John's step-father encouraged him to do when he first joined the agency as a Maine game warden.

John previously wrote two books, *Suddenly, The Cider Didn't Taste So Good* and *This Cider Still Tastes Funny. Deer Diaries--Tales of a Maine Game Warden,* is his third. Each of them are filled with actual events written up as short stories. The tales, mostly humorous, are some of the young game warden's most memorable experiences.

John lives with his wonderful wife, Judy, in Brooks, Maine.

Remembering Those
at the End of Their Watch

I'd like to end this writing, shifting from the many personal encounters that made my career so enjoyable, to one with a solemn remembrance. I want to forever preserve the memory of my colleagues who have made the ultimate sacrifice. Their final story is far from being humorous. Instead, it tells of how quickly the dangerous careers we chose could have taken any one of us at any given time.

Since the beginning of Warden Service fifteen of my fellow brothers have died in the line of duty. Their sudden and tragic deaths were a sharp reminder to us in the field that at any moment we too could be the next law enforcement officer to have our so-called "end of watch."

Since 1880, the Maine Warden Service tragically lost more of its men than any other law enforcement agency within the state. I want to dedicate this book and the many pleasant memories within it to the families and friends of those who made the ultimate sacrifice. They too had their fond stories and memories to tell, but sadly they never got to share them.

Lest we forget, these men rendered admirable service to the citizens of Maine and demonstrated relentless dedication to protecting wildlife in our great state.

The following men, sadly, have ended their watch:

Warden Lyman O. Hill and
Deputy Warden Charles W. Niles _Monday November 08, 1886_
Game Warden Lyman O. Hill and Deputy Warden Charles W. Niles were shot and killed while attempting to arrest two poachers on the Machias River. Deputy Warden Niles and Warden Hill had been tracking the poachers, who had been

using a team of dogs to run deer, for about ten days. When they finally approached the men an argument broke out. As Deputy Warden Niles took off his coat in order to take hold of the poachers' dog, one of the poachers pulled out a double-barrel shotgun and opened fire. Deputy Warden Niles and Warden Hill were both killed instantly.

Warden Arthur G. Deag   *Tuesday July 19, 1921*
Game Warden Arthur Deag drowned after his canoe capsized at Pockwockamus Falls on the West Branch of the Penobscot River. It is believed that the opening of Rip Dam caused a surge of water that overturned the canoe. Warden Deag struck his head on a hard object in the water and drowned. The son of the commissioner of Department of Inland Fisheries and Wildlife was riding in the canoe with Warden Deag but he was able to make it to safety.

Warden Leslie Robinson   *Saturday October 08, 1921*
Game Warden Leslie Robinson was killed in an automobile accident while on patrol near Ragged Lake in the Ripogenus area. His car overturned during a severe snowstorm. His partner was not seriously injured in the accident.

Wardens David F. Brown & Mertley E. Johnson
                                   Saturday November 11, 1922
Game Warden David Brown and Game Warden Mertley Johnston were shot and killed while working illegal beaver trapping near the Big Bog Dam on the North Branch of the Penobscot River. After shooting both wardens the Canadian suspect placed their bodies under the ice. Their bodies weren't located until May 22, 1923.

Warden Lee H. Parker   *Thursday September 01, 1927*
Deputy Warden Lee Parker was shot and killed after stopping a vehicle that contained four subjects who were spotlighting deer

in Westfield. The passenger of the vehicle shot Deputy Warden in the chest at point blank range. The suspect was apprehended and charged with murder. Deputy Warden Parker was survived by his wife and five children.

Warden Jean Baptiste Jalbert   _Saturday May 13, 1933_
Game Warden Jean Baptiste Jalbert drowned when his canoe capsized on the St. Francis River. The river was full of logs as a result of the spring log drive. The canoe struck one of the logs and overturned, throwing Warden Jalbert into the water.

Warden Robert L. Moore   _Tuesday October 22, 1935_
Warden Supervisor Robert Moore was killed in an automobile accident at Mayfield Crossing near Bingham. At the time of the accident, Warden Moore was driving his specially modified vehicle along the railroad tracks. As he approached a blind crossing his vehicle was struck by a sedan.

Warden Randall E. Shelley   _Monday June 03, 1946_
Game Warden Randall Shelley suffered a fatal heart attack while attempting to free his vehicle after it became stuck. He and his partner were patrolling the Moxie-Jackman area when the incident occurred.

Warden George E. Townsend   _Monday August 27, 1956_
Game Warden Pilot George Townsend was killed when the plane he was piloting crashed into Maranacook Lake shortly after taking off from its base in nearby Tallwood. A department biologist was also killed in this accident. Warden Townsend was survived by his wife, Louise, and his two sons, David and Steven.

Warden R. Lyle Frost Jr.   _Monday July 01, 1968_
Game Warden Lyle Frost was killed in an explosion while blowing up beaver dams in Franklin.

Warden Richard E. Varney   _Wednesday September 27, 1972_
Game Warden Pilot Richard Varney drowned after his helicopter crashed into Maranacook Lake. He had just taken off from the lake base when the helicopter experienced a malfunction and crashed. He was able to exit the wreckage but drowned before rescuers could make it to his location.

Warden William F. Hanrahan   _Saturday November 21, 1992_
Game Warden William Hanrahan suffered a fatal heart attack while investigating reports of drunk hunters in the woods near Starks. Warden Hanrahan had served with the Maine Department of Inland Fisheries and Wildlife Warden Service for 15 years. He was survived by his wife, daughter, and three sons.

Warden Daryl R. Gordon   _Thursday March 24, 2011_
Game Warden Daryl Gordon was killed in a plane crash in a remote area on the frozen Clear Lake in Piscataquis County. He was flying a department-owned Cessna 185 when it crashed sometime during the evening of March 24, 2011. A massive search was launched and wreckage, along with Warden Gordon's body, were located the following morning at approximately 9 am. Warden Gordon had served with the Maine Warden Service for 25 years. He was survived by his wife and two adult children.

All of these men made the ultimate sacrifice. Their names are forever inscribed upon the granite monument Fallen Officers Memorial located in Augusta, Maine. Personally, I recall my own great relationship with four of these men.
Warden George Townsend was a close family friend. As a youngster growing up along the shores of Mousam Lake in southern Maine, I vividly recall watching Pilot Townsend as he

landed his plane on the lake by our house, a location where he kept it overnight when he was in the area flying the local wardens around their districts. As George taxied on the ice to where my brother and I were ice skating, he graciously offered to take us up for our very first airplane ride.

George was a good friend of the family. We often vacationed in Rangeley during the summer, the place where George called his home. We shared many a good moment with George, his wife, Louise, and their two sons David and Steve. I can honestly say that it was George and his brother wardens who incited my desire of one day becoming a Maine game warden. His sudden death was a tragic loss for this youngster who had yet to join the force.

Warden Pilot Richard Varney - Prior to my becoming a warden, I had the opportunity to fly with him for my second ever plane ride when he flew my stepfather, Verne Walker, and I was invited to go along. That dream of becoming one of them was building with each chance meeting I had. Our friendship was strengthened when Dick assumed the responsibility for flying my patrol area in 1970, just as I was starting my young career. We certainly shared many great laughs between us prior to that fateful day when he received his "end of watch." One of those episodes I wrote about in great detail which brought tears to his eyes and a slight bit of embarrassment to yours truly. I will never forget those days nor the great men whose careers I wanted to follow.

Warden Bill Hanrahan was assigned to the same division as me. We worked several details together during our careers. His "end of watch" was yet another reminder of how quickly those that we love and respect can be gone in the blink of an eye.

The latest victim to receive the end of watch, **Warden Daryl Gordon**, worked a district north of mine. While we didn't share a lot of time together, he was among the very best at what he did. His faith in God and his dedication to the agency were second to none.

All of these heroes may be gone, but for this old retiree their memories will live forever. Like the many stories I've shared here, each of them had his own similar tales and adventures. We all did! One can only hope this list of fallen officers will be the last. But we know in all likelihood at some point in time other names will be added and yet other sacrifices will be made. It's the nature of the great career we chose.